Travaux pratiques de grammaire

HOLT, RINEHART AND WINSTON

A Harcourt Classroom Education Company

Austin • New York • Orlando • Atlanta • San Francisco • Boston • Dallas • Toronto • London

Cover Photo/Illustration Credits:
Illustration: Jean-Jacques Larrière

Printed in the United States of America

ISBN 0-03-064993-5

6 7 8 024 07 06 05 04

Contents

Nom ____________________ Classe ____________ Date ______________

Faisons connaissance!

PREMIERE ETAPE

When you meet people, you'll want to greet them, ask their names, and talk about how you're feeling. To ask someone's age and give yours, you'll want to know some numbers.

Greetings and telling how you feel

1 Circle the expression in each list that doesn't belong because of its meaning.

1. Au revoir.
   A tout à l'heure.
   Bonjour.
2. Tchao.
   Pas mal.
   Au revoir.
3. A bientôt.
   Bof.
   Tchao.
4. Pas mal.
   Super!
   Comme ci comme ça.
5. Très bien.
   Pas terrible.
   Salut.
6. Super!
   Pas mal.
   Tchao.

VOCABULAIRE Numbers 0–20

2 Solve the math problems below and fill in the puzzle with your answers.

HORIZONTALEMENT

5. Quinze moins *(minus)* six font *(equals)*...
6. Douze et *(plus)* sept font...
8. Dix moins dix font...
9. Dix-huit moins cinq font...
12. Onze et quatre font...
13. Treize moins neuf font...
14. Un et deux font...

VERTICALEMENT

1. Deux et quatre font...
2. Six et dix font...
3. Huit moins sept font...
4. Neuf et cinq font...
6. Onze et un font...
7. Treize et cinq font...
10. Quinze et cinq font...
11. Vingt moins douze font...

3 Write the number that would come next in each of these series.

1. dix, douze, quatorze, ______
2. neuf, douze, quinze, ______
3. zéro, cinq, dix, ______
4. dix-huit, seize, quatorze, ______
5. sept, huit, dix, treize, ______
6. seize, quinze, treize, ______

COMMENT DIT-ON... ? Giving your name and age

4 Francine is getting to know her new classmates. Match her questions with the responses her classmates give.

______ 1. Comment ça va?
______ 2. Tu t'appelles comment?
______ 3. Elle s'appelle comment?
______ 4. Il s'appelle comment?
______ 5. Tu as quel âge?

a. Je m'appelle Magali.
b. Comme ci comme ça.
c. Paul.
d. A demain.
e. Julie.
f. Quatorze ans.

5 Jérôme and Luc are talking before class. Unscramble their conversation by numbering the lines in the correct order.

______ — Comme ci comme ça. Et toi, ça va?
______ — Ça va?
______ — Bonjour. Je m'appelle Jérôme.
______ — Très bien, merci.
______ — Et moi, je m'appelle Luc.
______ — Bonjour.

6 Paméla and Frédéric are introducing themselves on the first day of class. Complete their conversation.

— Salut. (1) ______ m'appelle Paméla. Et toi? Tu t'appelles (2) ______?
— Je (3) ______ Frédéric.
— Tu as (4) ______ âge?
— (5) ______ seize ans. Et (6) ______?
— J'ai quinze (7) ______.

DEUXIEME ETAPE

To express likes, dislikes, and preferences, you'll need to be able to name some things you like and don't like. You'll also need to know how to make a sentence negative and how to use definite articles.

Note de Grammaire Using **ne... pas**

To make a verb like **aimer** negative, put **ne (n')... pas** around the verb.

J'aime la pizza. → Je **n'**aime **pas** la pizza.
Tu aimes le chocolat? → Tu **n'**aimes **pas** le chocolat?
Je préfère les escargots. → Je **ne** préfère **pas** les escargots.

Ne becomes **n'** before a word that begins with a vowel sound.

7 Your teacher made a list of what your classmates like and dislike. However, she was mistaken about several students. Correct her statements by making each sentence negative.

EXAMPLE Isabelle aime la plage. Non, Isabelle n'aime pas la plage.

1. Sabine aime les magasins. ______
2. Henri adore le français. ______
3. Didier aime les concerts. ______
4. Sylvain adore les vacances. ______
5. Raymond aime le cinéma. ______
6. Francine préfère le ski. ______
7. Paul aime le football. ______

8 François is very hard to please and doesn't like anything! Tell how he would answer these questions, using **ne (n')... pas** in your responses.

EXAMPLE Tu aimes la pizza? Non, je n'aime pas la pizza.

1. Tu aimes l'anglais? ______
2. Tu aimes le sport? ______
3. Tu aimes le chocolat? ______
4. Tu aimes les hamburgers? ______
5. Tu aimes la télévision? ______
6. Tu aimes les maths? ______
7. Tu aimes les examens? ______

VOCABULAIRE Likes and dislikes

9 Draw a line to match each item on the left with its equivalent on the right.

1. le vélo	beach
2. la plage	movie
3. le magasin	vacation
4. la glace	ice cream
5. les escargots	biking
6. l'ami	French fries
	snails
	friend
	store

10 Choose the item that best completes each of these sentences from the box below.

le français, la plage, le cinéma, le magasin, le vélo, les hamburgers

1. Paul aime beaucoup les fast-foods. Il aime les frites, la pizza et _______________.
2. Caroline aime l'école. Elle aime bien l'anglais, mais elle préfère _______________.
3. Joseph déteste le sport. Il n'aime pas _______________!

11 Write the words below in the appropriate categories.

le ski, le chocolat, le cinéma, les escargots, le français, les examens, le magasin, la glace, le vélo, les maths, le football, les frites

SPORTS	FOOD	SCHOOL	PLACES

Grammaire Definite articles

There are four ways to say *the* in French.

Before a masculine singular noun that begins with a consonant, use **le: le cinéma**
Before a feminine singular noun that begins with a consonant, use **la: la glace**
Before most singular nouns that begin with a vowel sound, use **l': l'école**
Before a plural noun, use **les: les examens**

12 Fill in the blanks with the correct definite article.

1. ____________ ski
2. ____________ vélo
3. ____________ pizza
4. ____________ école
5. ____________ escargots
6. ____________ chocolat
7. ____________ vacances
8. ____________ glace

13 Aurélie and her friend Sébastien are talking about their likes and dislikes. Complete their conversation with the correct definite articles.

AURELIE Salut, Sébastien! Dis, tu aimes **(1)** ____________ football?

SEBASTIEN Non, j'aime mieux **(2)** ____________ vélo. Et toi, tu aimes **(3)** ____________ sport?

AURELIE Oui, beaucoup. J'aime aussi **(4)** ____________ école. J'aime bien **(5)** ____________ maths, mais je préfère **(6)** ____________ français.

SEBASTIEN Moi aussi, j'aime **(7)** ____________ école, mais je n'aime pas **(8)** ____________ examens. Par contre, j'adore **(9)** ____________ vacances!

AURELIE Moi aussi. Tu aimes **(10)** ____________ plage?

SEBASTIEN Bien sûr!

14 Complete these statements by telling what items you like and dislike in each category.

1. *(food)* J'aime ____________________
   mais je n'aime pas ____________________.
2. *(sports)* J'aime ____________________
   mais je n'aime pas ____________________.
3. *(school)* J'aime ____________________
   mais je n'aime pas ____________________.
4. *(activities)* J'aime ____________________
   mais je n'aime pas ____________________.

TROISIEME ETAPE

To tell whether you and your friends like or dislike certain activities, you'll need to know the names of activities and how to use subject pronouns and -**er** verbs.

VOCABULAIRE Activities

15 Read Fabienne's letter to her new pen pal. Then, decide whether the statements that follow are true or false.

Bruno,

Bonjour! Ça va? Tu aimes le sport? Moi, j'adore le sport. J'aime bien nager et faire du vélo, mais j'aime mieux le ski. J'aime aussi écouter de la musique rock et parler au téléphone. Mais je n'aime pas regarder la télé. C'est nul! Et toi, qu'est-ce que tu aimes faire? Tchao!

Fabienne

__________ 1. Fabienne enjoys listening to rock music.

__________ 2. Fabienne doesn't like swimming.

__________ 3. She prefers skiing over other sports.

__________ 4. Fabienne enjoys watching television.

__________ 5. She enjoys talking on the phone.

16 Answer the following questions using the activities from the box below. Some activities may be used more than once.

regarder la télé
nager
parler au téléphone
étudier
faire de l'équitation
lire
faire le ménage

1. Which activities might you want to do in a quiet place?
____
____

2. Which activities involve a lot of movement?
____
____

3. Which activities do you usually do indoors?
____
____

17 Cédric is planning activities to do with his friends. From his notes, write down in French one activity each friend might like to do.

EXAMPLE Patrick — aime Céline Dion écouter de la musique

1. Aurélie — aime bien faire du sport _______________
2. Nadine — aime l'école _______________
3. Daniel — aime les vacances _______________
4. Edouard — adore la plage _______________

Grammaire Subject pronouns

Read the following sentences: Michel aime la glace. **Il** aime aussi les frites.

In the second sentence, **il** replaces Michel because it's the subject pronoun you use to replace something that is masculine and singular.

- The subject pronouns in French are:

je	*(I)*	**nous**	*(we)*
tu	*(you)*	**vous**	*(you)*
il	*(he* or *it)*	**ils**	*(they)*
elle	*(she* or *it)*	**elles**	*(they)*

- You change **je** to **j'** before a vowel sound.
- **Tu** and **vous** both mean *you*. Use **tu** with a friend, a family member, or someone your own age or younger. Use **vous** with more than one person or with an adult who isn't a family member.
- **Ils** and **elles** both mean *they*. Use **elles** to refer to a group of females. Use **ils** to refer to a group of males or a group of males and females together.

Julie et Marie? **Elles** n'aiment pas faire les magasins.
David et Paul? **Ils** aiment mieux nager.
Mélanie et Raymond? **Ils** aiment le cinéma.

18 Answer these questions about what your classmates like and dislike. Replace the underlined portions with the appropriate subject pronouns.

EXAMPLE Nathalie aime nager? → Oui, elle aime nager.

1. Eric et Jean-Paul aiment faire de l'équitation?

   Oui, _______________.
2. Marie-Claire et Danielle aiment étudier?

   Non, _______________.
3. Bruno aime les vacances?

   Oui, _______________.
4. Florence aime faire les magasins?

   Non, _______________.

19 You're taking a survey to find out how many people enjoy sports. Would you use **tu** or **vous** to address these people? Why?

1. Your friend Harold: ______________ because ______________ .
2. Your friends Florence and Etienne: ______________ because ______________ .
3. Your mother: ______________ because ______________ .
4. Your parents: ______________ because ______________ .
5. Mr. Jones, your father's boss: ______________ because ______________ .
6. Your five-year-old neighbor: ______________ because ______________ .

-er verbs

All French verbs change form depending on the subject. To make the forms of the verb **aimer,** drop the -**er** from the infinitive **aimer** and add the endings shown below. Most regular -**er** verbs follow this pattern.

j'aim**e**	nous aim**ons**
tu aim**es**	vous aim**ez**
il/elle aim**e**	ils/elles aim**ent**

Remember that noun subjects take the same verb forms as their pronouns.

Céline aime la plage.	OR	**Elle** aime la plage.
Eric et Pedro aiment étudier.	OR	**Ils** aiment étudier.

20 Choose the correct completion for each of these sentences.

_____ 1. Nous...
_____ 2. Tu...
_____ 3. Nathan...
_____ 4. Suzanne et Nicolas...
_____ 5. J'...
_____ 6. Vous...

a. aime l'anglais, mais il préfère le français.
b. adores dormir.
c. aiment parler au téléphone.
d. adorons faire de l'équitation.
e. aimez sortir avec les copains.
f. aime étudier.

21 You're writing the results of a survey you took to find out what teenagers like and dislike. Complete each sentence with the correct form of the verb in parentheses.

1. Eric et Michèle ______________ (aimer) danser.
2. Madame Duvalle et moi, nous ______________ (adorer) lire.
3. Caroline, Lise et Nathalie ______________ (aimer) faire du sport.
4. Serge ______________ (adorer) faire de l'équitation.
5. Stéphanie ______________ (aimer) écouter de la musique.

Nom ______________________ Classe ______________ Date ______________

22 Cross out the extra letters in the boxes to reveal the correct form of the verb for each of the sentences below.

1. Robert | S A E I F G M W E R | (aimer) faire le ménage.
2. Mes amis | A X P I W M E H G N O T | (aimer) bien parler au téléphone.
3. Vous | Q A D X C E O R F D E R Z | (adorer) faire les magasins.
4. Tu | P R A I M R E R E Z S | (aimer) mieux le ski ou le vélo?
5. Tu | S A D O W R Q E Z S P | (adorer) voyager, non?
6. Nous | Y E O A M I N M E O N T S | (aimer) danser.
7. Vous | V W A I Z E M S E Z P | (aimer) lire?

23 Unscramble the fragments below to create five complete sentences that tell what these people like, dislike, or prefer. Remember to put **aimer** in the correct form.

1. aimer / Nathalie / étudier / bien

____

2. aimer / Jérôme / vacances / les / et / Catherine / mieux

____

3. je (j') / pas / danser / ne (n') / aimer

____

4. nous / pas / ne (n') / le / faire / aimer / ménage

____

5. foot / ne (n') / tu / au / aimer / jouer / pas

____

24 List three things or activities you like and two you dislike.

______________________ ______________________

______________________ ______________________

____

Nom ____________________ Classe ____________ Date ____________

CHAPITRE 2

Vive l'école!

PREMIERE ETAPE

To agree and disagree about your opinions of classes, you'll need to use the names of some school subjects. You might also want to know how to contradict a negative statement or question.

VOCABULAIRE School subjects

1 You dropped your backpack and all your books are scattered on the floor. Choose the class each book is for, based on its title.

______ 1. *Chemistry: Visualizing Matter*

______ 2. *Elements of Literature*

______ 3. *Allez, viens!*

______ 4. *The American Nation*

______ 5. *Introduction to Algebra*

______ 6. *Modern Biology*

a. algèbre
b. histoire
c. chimie
d. chorale
e. français
f. anglais
g. biologie

2 Some French students made lists of the classes they have on Monday. Read their lists and then complete each statement that follows with the correct student's name.

Julien —	Francine —	Ahmed —	Julie —
français	anglais	maths	anglais
biologie	chimie	français	musique
EPS	maths	DPS	chorale
musique	arts plastiques	chorale	chimie
histoire	EPS	chimie	maths

1. ____________ has math, English, gym, art, and chemistry.
2. ____________ has music, choir, chemistry, English, and math.
3. ____________ has choir, health, math, chemistry, and French.
4. ____________ has history, French, biology, music, and gym.

3 For each of the groups below, circle the word that doesn't belong.

1. l'élève
   le professeur
   le latin
2. l'algèbre
   la musique
   la géométrie
3. la chimie
   la biologie
   l'EPS
4. les devoirs
   la chorale
   la danse
5. les sciences naturelles
   l'histoire
   la physique
6. l'allemand
   l'espagnol
   les arts plastiques

4 Your French pen pal will be spending a year in the United States. Give him an idea of what he can study at your school by listing in French the subjects offered in each of these areas of study.

1. SCIENCES: ____________________
2. MATHEMATICS: ____________________
3. FOREIGN LANGUAGES: ____________________
4. FINE ARTS: ____________________

Note de Grammaire **Si** versus **oui**

There are two ways to say *yes* in French.

Use **oui** to respond affirmatively to a statement or question.

— Frédéric aime la biologie?
— **Oui,** il aime beaucoup la biologie.

Use **si** to contradict a negative statement or question. To emphasize the contradiction, use **mais si.**

— Michel n'aime pas la chimie?
— **Si,** il aime beaucoup.

— Tu n'aimes pas le français?
— **Mais si,** j'adore le français.

5 Marta, a new student, doesn't know your friends very well yet. Contradict or confirm her impressions, using **si** or **oui** in your answers.

1. — Elizabeth aime la prof de maths?
   — ________, elle adore Madame Guy.
2. — David n'aime pas le français?
   — ________, il adore le français.
3. — Thi n'aime pas la chorale?
   — ________, elle aime bien la chorale.
4. — Hélène et Paméla aiment les arts plastiques?
   — ________, elles aiment les arts plastiques.
5. — Pedro et Magali n'aiment pas les devoirs?
   — ________, ils aiment les devoirs.
6. — Annick aime la danse?
   — ________, elle aime beaucoup la danse.
7. — Tarek et Eric n'aiment pas danser?
   — ________, ils adorent danser.

DEUXIEME ETAPE

To ask for and give information about your schedule, you'll need to know the verb **avoir** and some adverbs, the days of the week, the numbers from 21 to 59, and how to tell time.

VOCABULAIRE Expressions of time

6 Find five expressions of time in the puzzle below and then list them in the blanks.

M B R A D F P L D W I K A '
A U – P M R O G V U S U D A
I A P O ' I È L H Q L – A O
N G W P N B U ' N O Q J E L
T Q A U E I D M W H N B V I
E T J A P R È S – M I D I D
N E O S U – N R Q U J I A C
A M – O R J I P J T N R T X
N B J J L G X R U D I H P N
T U M H T I D L I – T Q D I
A X D E M A I N G P A U R È
I Z D R C E S X A Z M U P R

____

____

____

____

____

Grammaire The verb avoir

The verb **avoir** *(to have)* is irregular. Here are its forms:

j'**ai**	nous **avons**
tu **as**	vous **avez**
il/elle **a**	ils/elles **ont**

When you use **avoir** to tell what classes you have, you don't use the definite articles **le, la, l'**, or **les.**

Il **a** chimie. *He has chemistry.*
Nous **avons** arts plastiques. *We have art class.*

7 You and your friends are talking about your school schedules. Choose the correct completion for each of the statements below.

_______ **1.** Sabine et Paul...

_______ **2.** Moi, j'...

_______ **3.** Danielle...

_______ **4.** Eric et moi, nous...

_______ **5.** Vous...

a. a chimie et maths le matin.

b. avez physique demain.

c. ai latin cet après-midi.

d. avons sport aujourd'hui.

e. ont allemand maintenant.

8 Nicole and her friends are telling one another when they have various classes. Complete their statements with the correct forms of the verb **avoir.**

1. «Pauline et Marie-Hélène ____________ chimie et maths le matin.»
2. «Henri ____________ sport, et moi, j'____________ anglais le matin.»
3. «L'après-midi, vous ____________ quoi?»
4. «Après le déjeuner, nous ____________ tous histoire.»
5. «Et toi, David, tu ____________ quels cours l'après-midi?»

9 Unscramble these sentences. Use the correct form of the verb **avoir** in each one.

1. avoir / sciences nat / aujourd'hui / nous

   ____.
2. j' / algèbre / le / avoir / matin

   ____.
3. avoir / tu / l' / quels / après-midi / cours

   ____?
4. maintenant / avoir / vous / espagnol

   ____.
5. Martin / arts / avoir / demain / plastiques

   ____.

VOCABULAIRE Days of the week

10 Unscramble these days of the week. Then, rewrite them in order the French way, beginning with Monday.

1. C E N I M A D H ____________________
2. I J D U E ____________________
3. D R M A I ____________________
4. I D A S E M ____________________
5. L D N I U ____________________
6. D I E N D V R E ____________________
7. I D R M E C E R ____________________

____________, ____________, ____________, ____________,

____________, ____________, ____________

Nom ______________ Classe ______________ Date ______________

EMPLOI DU TEMPS **DUCHARME Marion**

	LUNDI	MARDI	MERCREDI	JEUDI	VENDREDI	SAMEDI
8H30	Biologie	Maths	Physique	EPS	Etude	Français
9H30	Anglais	Latin	Histoire	Biologie	Histoire	Maths
10H30	EPS	EPS	Musique	Chimie	Latin	Latin
11H30			DEJEUNER			
13H30	Français	Anglais		Français	Maths	
14H30	Musique	Biologie	LIBRE	Physique	Chimie	LIBRE
15H30	Histoire	Chimie		Anglais	Physique	
16H30	Chimie	Chorale		Français	Chorale	

11 Use Marion's schedule to answer these questions in English.

1. On what days does Marion have chemistry? ______________
2. On what days does she have music? ______________
3. On what days does she have English? ______________
4. What two classes does Marion attend only in the morning? ______________

12 Marion and her friend Jocelyne are comparing their schedules. Complete their conversation, using Marion's schedule above.

JOCELYNE Alors, Marion, tu as quoi le lundi matin?

MARION (1) J'ai ______________.

JOCELYNE Et le lundi après-midi, tu as quoi?

MARION (2) J'ai ______________.

JOCELYNE Moi, j'ai sport le mardi et le vendredi matin. Et toi, tu as sport le matin ou l'après-midi?

MARION (3) J'ai sport ______________.

JOCELYNE Tu as français quand?

MARION (4) J'ai français ______________.

VOCABULAIRE Numbers 21–59

13 Your friend asked you for today's homework assignments. Write the words for the page numbers you would tell her to read.

1. histoire, p. 46
2. géométrie, p. 24
3. sciences nat, p. 38
4. anglais, p. 59

1. ______________
2. ______________
3. ______________
4. ______________

14 Write out in French the number that would come next in each of the series below.

1. trente, trente-cinq, quarante... ______
2. vingt, trente, quarante... ______
3. six, douze, vingt-quatre... ______
4. quarante et un, quarante-quatre, quarante-huit... ______
5. cinquante-neuf, cinquante, quarante et un... ______

COMMENT DIT-ON...? Telling time

15 Match Martha's class times to the correct numerals on the right.

______ 1. J'ai anglais à huit heures cinquante.
______ 2. J'ai français à treize heures vingt-cinq.
______ 3. J'ai maths à quatorze heures quarante.
______ 4. On a récréation à quinze heures trente-cinq.
______ 5. On a histoire à quinze heures cinquante-cinq.

a. 13h40
b. 15h35
c. 14h40
d. 14h30
e. 15h55
f. 8h50
g. 13h25

16 What time do these clocks show? Write out the times in French.

8:25	13:45	11:10	19:04	23:30
1.	2.	3.	4.	5.

1. ______
2. ______
3. ______
4. ______
5. ______

17 Write complete sentences telling when these people have the following classes.

EXAMPLE vous / anglais / 16h25 → Vous avez anglais à seize heures vingt-cinq.

1. Eric / biologie / 8h00 ______
2. je / maths / 9h45 ______
3. nous / français / 11h30 ______
4. tu / EPS / 13h15 ______
5. Zoé et Luc / histoire / 14h50 ______

Nom ____________________ Classe ____________ Date ____________

TROISIEME ETAPE

To say how you feel about your classes, you need to be able to express favorable and unfavorable opinions and indifference.

Using adjectives to express opinions

18 Céline and Didier are talking about their classes. Read their conversation and circle the expressions that express favorable opinions. Then, underline the expressions that express unfavorable opinions.

CELINE Comment tu trouves les sciences nat?
DIDIER C'est génial! Et toi, comment tu trouves ça?
CELINE C'est intéressant. J'aime bien les sciences. Et l'anglais, tu aimes ça?
DIDIER Non, c'est pas super. Et toi, tu aimes l'histoire?
CELINE Oui, c'est passionnant!
DIDIER Moi, je n'aime pas ça. C'est barbant.

CHAPITRE 2 Troisième étape

19 These students are discussing how they feel about their classes. Based on their opinions, tell whether the students like **(L)**, dislike **(D)**, or feel indifferent **(I)** about their classes.

_____ 1. La géo, c'est super!

_____ 2. La biologie, c'est pas terrible.

_____ 3. C'est nul, les maths.

_____ 4. C'est passionnant, l'histoire.

_____ 5. La chimie, c'est pas mal.

_____ 6. Le français, c'est génial!

20 You want to be a scientist and work in France. Your schedule is identical to Marion Ducharme's schedule on page 14. Your favorite classes are those that prepare you for your future career as a scientist. Look at the schedule for Thursdays, then write five sentences telling at what time you have each class and your opinion of each class.

EXAMPLE A huit heures trente, j'ai EPS. C'est pas mal.

____
____
____
____
____
____

CHAPITRE 3

Tout pour la rentrée

PREMIERE ETAPE

To make and respond to requests and to talk about what you and others need at school, you'll need to use the indefinite articles and school supplies.

VOCABULAIRE School supplies

1 Sylvie and her classmates made lists of the supplies they need for school. Read their lists and then answer the questions that follow.

Sylvie :
une calculatrice
un stylo
un cahier
une gommme
des crayons

Ahmed :
un classeur
un sac à dos
un cahier
une trousse
un stylo

Danielle :
des crayons
des stylos
un cahier
des feuilles de papier
un taille-crayon

Bruno :
une calculatrice
un sac à dos
une règle
un taille-crayon
des stylos

Thi :
un stylo
une trousse
des crayons
un cahier
un sac à dos

Patricia :
un classeur
un cahier
un stylo
des feuilles de papier
une trousse

1. Who needs pencils? ______
2. Who needs a backpack? ______
3. Who needs a pencil case? ______
4. Who needs a binder? ______
5. Who needs a calculator? ______
6. Who needs a pencil sharpener? ______
7. Who needs a ruler? ______
8. Who needs an eraser? ______

2 Solve these riddles by choosing the appropriate answers from the box below.

un stylo	**une règle**	**un taille-crayon**	**des feuilles de papier**	
une gomme	**un classeur**	**un sac à dos**	**une trousse**	**une calculatrice**

1. ______________ Use me to measure things.
2. ______________ You need me when you make a mistake.
3. ______________ If you want to organize your papers, I can help.
4. ______________ I'll carry your books and supplies for you.
5. ______________ I can sharpen your pencils.
6. ______________ I'll carry your pencils and pens.

3 Write the French names for the supplies you might need for these classes.

1. l'algèbre ______________
2. les arts plastiques ______________
3. la géométrie ______________
4. l'histoire ______________

Grammaire The indefinite articles **un**, **une**, and **des**

You use indefinite articles to say *a, an,* or *some* before a noun.

Before . . .

a masculine noun, use **un:**	Il a **un** classeur.	*He has a notebook.*
a feminine noun, use **une:**	Il a **une** règle.	*He has a ruler.*
any plural noun, use **des:**	Il a **des** stylos.	*He has some pens.*

Change **un**, **une**, and **des** to **de (d')** after **ne... pas.**

Sylvie a **des** livres. → Sylvie n'a pas **de** livres.
J'ai **un** cahier. → Je n'ai pas **de** cahier.
J'ai **un** examen. → Je n'ai pas **d'**examen.

4 Complete Magali's shopping list with the correct indefinite article **un**, **une**, or **des.**

1. ________ stylo
2. ________ cahier
3. ________ trousse
4. ________ vidéocassettes
5. ________ classeurs
6. ________ gomme
7. ________ crayons
8. ________ sac à dos

5 Your computer has a bug in it. It keeps deleting the indefinite articles! Complete the sentences by filling in the blanks with **un, une,** or **des.**

1. DAVID A ________ RÈGLE, ________ CLASSEUR ET ________ TROUSSE.
2. IL ME FAUT ________ STYLO ET ________ CAHIER POUR L'ANGLAIS.
3. MARIE-HÉLÈNE A ________ FEUILLES DE PAPIER, ________ TAILLE-CRAYON ET ________ TROUSSE.
4. POUR LES MATHS, HENRI A ________ CALCULATRICE, ________ CRAYONS ET ________ GOMME.

6 José and Gabrielle are talking about what they need for school. Complete their conversation with **un, une, des,** or **de (d').**

GABRIELLE José, qu'est-ce qu'il te faut pour la rentrée?

JOSE Il me faut **(1)** ________ trousse et **(2)** ________ stylos. Et toi, qu'est-ce qu'il te faut?

GABRIELLE Ben, moi, je n'ai pas **(3)** ________ trousse. Il me faut aussi **(4)** ________ sac à dos, **(5)** ________ calculatrice et **(6)** ________ crayons.

JOSE Ah oui! Moi aussi, il me faut **(7)** ________ calculatrice. Tu as **(8)** ________ feuilles de papier?

GABRIELLE Non, je n'ai pas **(9)** ________ feuilles. Il me faut beaucoup de choses!

7 Some of Madame Dupont's students aren't prepared for class today. Write their responses to her questions.

EXAMPLE — Vous avez des livres, Christophe et Hafaïdh?
— Non, nous n'avons pas de livres.

1. — Vous avez des stylos, Serge et Paméla?
   — Non, ____.
2. — Tu as des feuilles de papier, Antoine?
   — Oui, ____.
3. — Tu as une règle, Odile?
   — Non, ____.
4. — Vous avez des crayons, Nadine et Paul?
   — Non, ____.
5. — Viviane, tu as une calculatrice?
   — Oui, ____.
6. — Hichem et Amadou, vous avez des gommes?
   — Non, ____.

Nom ______________________ Classe ______________ Date ______________

DEUXIEME ETAPE

To tell what you'd like and what you'd like to buy, you'll need to name some items and point them out, using demonstrative adjectives. You'll also want to know the colors and how to use adjectives correctly.

VOCABULAIRE At the store

8 Try to guess the items from the clues given. Then, decode your responses to figure out what Patricia is buying Robert for his birthday.

1. You can play this in your stereo.
   ___ ___ ___ ___ ___ ___ ___ ___
   5 3 10 10 1 7 7 1
2. You wear this on your wrist.
   ___ ___ ___ ___ ___ ___ ___ ___
   8 11 3 5 1 9 1 7
3. You wear this when it's cold.
   ___ ___ ___ ___ — ___ ___ ___ ___
   2 6 9 9 12 15 1 11
4. You tell time with this.
   ___ ___ ___ ___ ___ ___
   4 12 14 7 11 1
5. You carry money in this.
   ___ ___ ___ ___ ___ ___ ___ ___ ___ ___ ___ ___
   2 12 11 7 1 17 1 6 13 9 9 1

Patricia achète un : ___ ___ ___ ___ ___ ___
2 12 10 7 1 11

9 Your friend is asking you what gifts she should buy for Karine, Mai, Tanguy, and François. Suggest two gifts based on each person's interests.

une radio · un jean · une montre · un bracelet · un roman · un CD · un poster · un dictionnaire · un portefeuille · une cassette · un sweat-shirt · un magazine · des baskets · un ordinateur

1. *Karine aime la musique.*
   ____
   ____
2. *Tanguy aime le sport.*
   ____
   ____
3. *Mai aime les bijoux (jewelry).*
   ____
   ____
4. *François aime lire.*
   ____
   ____

CHAPITRE 3 Deuxième étape

Grammaire Demonstrative adjectives

To say *this, that, these,* or *those,* use a demonstrative adjective. The adjective you use depends on whether the noun you're referring to is masculine or feminine, singular or plural, and whether or not it begins with a vowel sound.

	MASCULINE	FEMININE
SINGULAR	**ce** roman	**cette** montre
(before a vowel sound)	**cet** ordinateur	**cette** école
PLURAL	**ces** livres	**ces** cassettes

When you want to specify *that* as opposed to *this,* add **-là** *(there)* to the end of the noun.

— Tu aimes **ce bracelet**? — Do you like *this* bracelet?
— Oui, mais je préfère **ce bracelet-là.** — Yes, but I prefer *that* bracelet.

10 Chantal and Pierre-Yves are looking for gifts for their friends and family. Complete their statements with **ce, cet, cette,** or **ces.**

1. J'aime bien ________ tee-shirts, mais j'aime mieux ________ pull-overs.
2. Je voudrais acheter ________ roman pour mon frère. Il aime lire. Et moi, comme j'adore la musique, je vais acheter ________ cassette de MC Solaar.
3. J'adore ________ montre. Elle est cool!
4. Pour mon père, je vais acheter ________ portefeuille.
5. Il me faut ________ ordinateur pour l'école.

11 Elise and Christian don't like the same things. Write Elise's responses to Christian's statements.

EXAMPLE — Tu aimes ce short?
— Non, mais j'aime ce short-là.

1. — Tu aimes ce bracelet?
— ________________________________
2. — Tu aimes cette montre?
— ________________________________
3. — Tu aimes ce jean?
— ________________________________
4. — Tu aimes ces baskets?
— ________________________________
5. — Tu aimes cet ordinateur?
— ________________________________

VOCABULAIRE Colors

12 What color(s) do you associate with the following items? Write your responses in French.

1. les bananes ______________________
2. les carottes ______________________
3. la salade ______________________
4. les zèbres ______________________
5. le drapeau *(flag)* américain ______________________

Grammaire Adjective agreement

In French, adjectives must agree in number (singular/plural) and gender (masculine/feminine) with the nouns they describe.

	MASCULINE	FEMININE
SINGULAR	un sac noir	une trousse noir**e**
PLURAL	des sacs noir**s**	des trousses noir**es**

To make most adjectives feminine, you add an **–e** to the masculine form. However, if the masculine singular form ends in an unaccented **–e**, you don't add another **–e.**

le sac vert → la trousse vert**e**
le bracelet rouge → la montre rouge

To make most adjectives plural, you add an **–s** to both the masculine and feminine words. However, if the singular form ends in an **–s**, you don't add another **–s.**

la trousse bleue → les trousses bleue**s**
le sac gris → les sacs gris

13 Pauline wrote her mother a note telling what she'd like from the store, but she wasn't very specific. Her mother wants more details. Make Pauline's list more descriptive by adding the correct forms of the adjectives in parentheses.

Je voudrais des baskets (1) __________ (noir), un short (2) __________ (noir), un tee-shirt (3) __________ (vert), un tee-shirt (4) __________ (rose), un jean (5) __________ (bleu), des stylos (6) __________ (bleu), des stylos (7) __________ (rouge), des trousses (8) __________ (gris) et un sac à dos (9) __________ (rouge).

Irregular adjectives

There are adjectives that don't follow the rules you've already learned. Some of these adjectives, like **blanc** and **violet**, follow a different pattern in the feminine form:

un tee-shirt blanc	une montre blanc**he**
des tee-shirts blancs	des montres blanc**hes**
un tee-shirt violet	une montre violet**te**
des tee-shirts violets	des montres violet**tes**

Other adjectives, such as **orange** and **marron**, never change form.

un tee-shirt orange	une montre orange
des tee-shirts orange	des montres orange
un tee-shirt marron	une montre marron
des tee-shirts marron	des montres marron

14 Your friend is going to France as a foreign exchange student. She wrote this list of items she would like to buy when she arrives, but she can't remember the French words for the colors of the items. Complete her list below with the correct French forms of the colors in parentheses.

1. des cahiers ____________ (brown)
2. une trousse ____________ (purple)
3. des stylos ____________ (blue)
4. des baskets ____________ (white)
5. des classeurs ____________ (white)
6. un jean ____________ (black)
7. des sweat-shirts ____________ (grey)
8. une règle ____________ (pink)

Position of adjectives

Have you noticed where adjectives usually appear in a French sentence?

Claire adore ces baskets **blanches!**
Je voudrais une trousse **marron.**

You place most adjectives, including colors, after the nouns they describe.

15 Rewrite these remarks, adding a color from the box below. Make all necessary changes.

vert marron violet blanc

1. J'adore ces bracelets! ____________
2. J'adore cette montre! ____________
3. Denis achète des baskets. ____________
4. J'aime bien ces tee-shirts. ____________

Nom ______________________ Classe ______________ Date ______________

TROISIEME ETAPE

In order to ask for prices, you'll need to know more numbers.

VOCABULAIRE Numbers from 60 to 999

16 You're working in a French store. Complete these price tags by filling in the correct numbers.

1. quatre-vingt-quatorze ______ €
2. sept cent dix ______ €
3. soixante-sept ______ €
4. cent cinquante-quatre

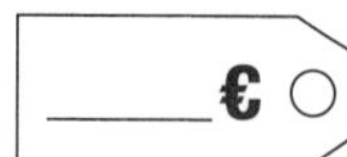

5. deux cents

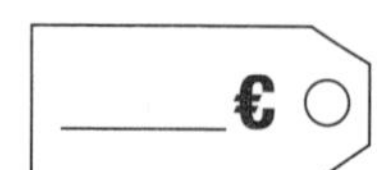

6. cent quarante et un

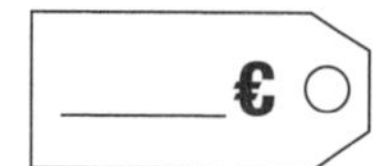

17 Write out the amount on each of these checks.

1. 71€ ____________________________________ euros
2. 549 € ____________________________________ euros
3. 101€ ____________________________________ euros
4. 92 € ____________________________________ euros

18 You're out shopping. Tell the salesperson that you want three items in the color of your choice at a reasonable price.

EXAMPLE <u>Je voudrais ce sac rouge à trente euros.</u>

jean, tee-shirt, montre, pull-over, bracelet, sac, baskets

violet, rouge, bleu, noir, vert, blanc, marron

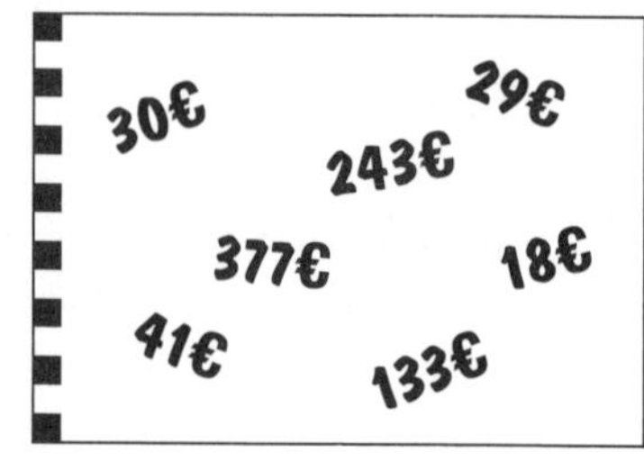

1. ____________________________________
____
2. ____________________________________
____
3. ____________________________________
____

Sports et passe-temps

PREMIERE ETAPE

To tell how much you like or dislike something, you'll need to use the names of some more activities and expressions with **faire** and **jouer.** To ask how much someone likes or dislikes something, you'll need to know how to form questions.

VOCABULAIRE Sports and hobbies

1 At the recreation center, you're in charge of suggesting activities that fit people's interests. Suggest two or three activities to your clients.

EXAMPLE Stéphane and Mai like team sports.
Vous pourriez... *(You could . . .)* jouer au football, jouer au base-ball ou jouer au hockey.

faire du patin à glace · faire du ski nautique · jouer au base-ball · faire du vélo · jouer au golf · jouer au tennis · faire de la vidéo · jouer à des jeux vidéo · faire de l'aérobic · jouer aux cartes · jouer au football · faire de la natation

1. Marc and Sophie like outdoor sports.
   Vous pourriez ________________.
2. Angélique likes water sports.
   Tu pourrais ________________.
3. Didier likes indoor activities, but not sports.
   Tu pourrais ________________.
4. Serge likes individual sports.
   Tu pourrais ________________.

2 While cleaning out the storage closet at the recreation center, you found these items. Write the sport or activity in French that you can do with the equipment.

1. helmet, knee pads, bike ________________
2. video camera, videocassettes ________________
3. bat, glove ________________
4. golf clubs, golf balls ________________
5. in-line skates, knee pads, helmet ________________

Grammaire Expressions with **faire** and **jouer**

- To say that you *play a sport or game,* use **jouer à** + the activity. The preposition **à** changes to **au** before a masculine singular noun that begins with a consonant.

  Marc joue **au** football après l'école.

  When the game or sport is plural, **à** becomes **aux.**

  Virginie joue **aux** cartes.

  It doesn't change before all other singular nouns.

- To say you *do an activity,* use **faire de** + the activity. **De** changes to **du** before a masculine singular noun and to **des** before a plural noun.

  Sophie aime faire **du** jogging.
  Henri aime faire **des** photos.

  It doesn't change before all other singular nouns.

  Pauline aime faire **de l'**aérobic.
  Guillaume aime faire **de la** natation.

3 Help Nathalie finish her list of favorite activities by adding the appropriate verbs.

J'aime

(1) ________ au tennis,
(2) ________ de l'aérobic,
(3) ________ de la photo,
(4) ________ au golf,
(5) ________ de la natation,
(6) ________ du vélo,
(7) ________ au volley,
(8) ________ du jogging et
(9) ________ aux cartes.

4 Pascal and Odile are discussing what they like to do on vacation. Complete their conversation with **jouer**, **faire**, or the appropriate form of **à** or **de**.

au	à la	à l'	jouer	du	de la	de l'	faire	des

PASCAL Dis, Odile, qu'est-ce que tu aimes faire pendant les vacances?

ODILE J'aime **(1)** ________ du vélo et **(2)** ________ natation. J'aime aussi jouer **(3)** ________ foot avec mes amis. Et toi, qu'est-ce que tu aimes faire?

PASCAL Moi, j'aime **(4)** ________ du roller en ligne. Ma sœur et moi, nous aimons aussi faire **(5)** ________ vidéo.

ODILE Tu aimes faire **(6)** ________ photo, non?

PASCAL Oui, bien sûr! Mais j'aime surtout **(7)** ________ au tennis.

ODILE Est-ce que tu aimes faire **(8)** ________ aérobic?

PASCAL Non, pas trop. J'aime mieux faire **(9)** ________ jogging.

Grammaire Question formation

Here are two ways to make yes-no questions:

1. You can raise the pitch of your voice at the end of the sentence.

   Tu aimes faire du patin à glace?

2. You can also add **est-ce que** before a statement and raise your voice at the end of the statement. When you hear **est-ce que**, you know you're going to hear a question.

   Est-ce que tu aimes faire du patin à glace?

5 A classmate has sent you an encoded note. First unscramble her questions. Then place a check mark next to the answer you'd give.

1. foot / tu / aimes / au / est-ce que / jouer

   ____?

   _____ Oui, j'aime beaucoup ça. _____ Non, je n'aime pas tellement ça.

2. natation / aimes / la / tu / de / faire / est-ce que

   ____?

   _____ Oui, j'aime beaucoup ça. _____ Non, je n'aime pas du tout ça.

3. du / faire / tu / est-ce que / nautique / aimes / ski

   ____?

   _____ Oui, j'aime beaucoup ça. _____ Non, je n'aime pas tellement ça.

4. jeux / tu / vidéo / à / aimes / est-ce que / jouer / des

   ____?

   _____ Oui, j'aime beaucoup ça. _____ Non, je n'aime pas du tout ça.

6 A reporter for the school newspaper is interviewing a young celebrity about her likes and dislikes. Based on the answers the celebrity gives, write the interviewer's questions, using **est-ce que.**

1. — ____?

   — Oui, j'aime bien ça. Je nage tous les jours.

2. — ____?

   — Oui, beaucoup! J'aime faire de la vidéo.

3. — ____?

   — Oui, j'aime beaucoup faire du patin le week-end.

4. — ____?

   — Non, je n'aime pas beaucoup jouer au hockey, mais je regarde quelquefois les matchs de hockey à la télé.

Nom ____________________ Classe ____________ Date ____________

DEUXIEME ETAPE

To talk about the sports and activities in which you do and do not participate, you'll need to know the verb **faire** and know how to use **de** in a negative sentence. You might also need to know how to describe the weather and name the seasons.

Note de Grammaire **De** after a negative

Du, de la, and **de l'** usually change to **de (d')** after a negative expression such as **ne... pas.**

Perrine fait **de l'**athlétisme, mais Luc ne fait pas **d'**athlétisme.
Marie fait **de la** vidéo. Moi, je ne fais pas **de** vidéo.

7 Sébastien and Mai are talking about the activities they like and dislike. Complete their conversation by circling the correct form of **de**.

— Dis, Sébastien, tu aimes faire **(1)** (du / de) roller, toi?

— Non, je ne fais pas **(2)** (du / de) roller. Mais j'aime faire **(3)** (du / de) patin à glace.

— Moi aussi! Qu'est-ce que tu fais après l'école? **(4)** (Du / De) jogging?

— Oui, je fais **(5)** (du / de) jogging. Je fais aussi **(6)** (de l' / d') aérobic.

— Moi non! Je ne fais pas **(7)** (de l' / d') aérobic. C'est trop dur!

— Tu aimes faire **(8)** (de la / de) vidéo?

— Non, je ne fais pas **(9)** (de la / de) vidéo. C'est barbant.

8 Write four sentences telling which of the activities below you do and which you don't do.

EXAMPLE Je fais du ski, mais je ne fais pas de vélo.

faire du patin à glace
faire du roller en ligne
faire du jogging
faire du ski
faire de l'équitation
faire du vélo
faire de l'athlétisme
faire de la vidéo
faire de l'aérobic
faire des photos
faire de la natation

1. ____________________

2. ____________________

3. ____________________

4. ____________________

Grammaire The verb faire

The verb **faire** is irregular. It has several different meanings, including *to do, to play,* and *to make.* Here are its forms:

je	**fais**	nous	**faisons**
tu	**fais**	vous	**faites**
il/elle/on	**fait**	ils/elles	**font**

Je **fais** mes devoirs. *I do (am doing) my homework.*
François **fait** du sport. *François plays sports.*

9 You and your friends are discussing your plans for the week. Complete these statements by filling in the correct subjects from the box on the left. Use each subject only once.

nous
Julien et Laurent
je
Francine et Marion
toi, tu
Elisabeth

1. Le lundi, ______________________ faisons du ski.
2. Le mardi, ______________________ fais de la natation. J'adore ça!
3. Le mercredi, ______________________ font du ski nautique. Elles adorent les sports nautiques.
4. Le jeudi, ______________________ fait du patin à glace.
5. Le vendredi, ______________________ font du théâtre. Ils aiment beaucoup le théâtre.
6. Le samedi, ______________________ fais du vélo.

10 Didier wrote a letter to his family telling them what he and his friends are doing at summer camp. Complete his letter by filling in the blanks with the correct forms of the verb **faire**.

Chers Papa et Maman,

Je (1) __________ beaucoup de choses ici! Le matin, je (2) __________ du jogging ou du vélo. L'après-midi, mes amis et moi, nous (3) __________ de la natation ou de l'équitation. Nathalie et Suzanne, elles (4) __________ du théâtre. Moi, je n'aime pas tellement le théâtre, mais j'aime (5) __________ de la vidéo. Et vous, qu'est-ce que vous (6) __________ en ce moment? A bientôt.

Bises,

Didier

Grammaire The pronoun **on**

The subject pronoun **on** usually means *we* in conversational French. In some situations, however, it can mean *they* or *you* when it refers to people in general.

On uses the same form of the verb as **il/elle.**

Après l'école, **on fait** de l'aérobic. *After school, we do aerobics.*
En France, **on joue** beaucoup au football. *In France, they play soccer a lot.*

11 Your pen pal wants to know about the activities people in the United States generally like to do. What are three activities you and your friends do?

faire du jogging
faire du roller
jouer au basket-ball
faire de la photo
jouer au foot
jouer à des jeux vidéo
faire de la vidéo
faire du vélo
jouer au volley-ball

Mes amis et moi, on ______________________________

____

____

____

____

VOCABULAIRE Weather expressions

12 Your French pen pal is visiting and isn't used to hearing temperatures given in degrees Fahrenheit. Help your friend by describing in French the weather indicated by each temperature.

1. 99° F ______________________________
2. 15° F ______________________________
3. 60° F ______________________________
4. 75° F ______________________________
5. 30° F ______________________________
6. 90° F ______________________________

Nom _______________ Classe _______________ Date _______________

VOCABULAIRE Months of the year

13 Look at the following chart from the newspaper and tell what the weather is like in the following cities.

Paris		59° F	Québec		30° F
Montpellier		75° F	Fort-de-France		85° F
Strasbourg		51° F	Abidjan		91° F

1. Paris _______________
2. Montpellier _______________
3. Fort-de-France _______________
4. Abidjan _______________
5. Québec _______________
6. Strasbourg _______________

14 Tell in French in which months the following holidays or events occur.

EXAMPLE Hanukkah en décembre

1. American Independence Day _______________
2. Christmas _______________
3. Cinco de mayo _______________
4. Father's Day _______________
5. Labor Day _______________
6. Martin Luther King Jr.'s Birthday _______________
7. Valentine's Day _______________
8. Thanksgiving _______________
9. St. Patrick's Day _______________
10. Mother's Day _______________
11. April Fool's Day _______________
12. First day of school _______________

Tu te rappelles? -er verbs

All regular -**er** verbs, like **jouer**, will follow the same pattern as the verb **aimer** that you learned in Chapter 1.

je	jou**e**	nous	jou**ons**
tu	jou**es**	vous	jou**ez**
il/elle/on	jou**e**	ils/elles	jou**ent**

15 Complete each sentence with the correct form of the verb in parentheses.

1. Nous ______________ (parler) français en classe.
2. Tu ______________ (aimer) faire du ski?
3. Nathalie et Paméla ______________ (jouer) au volley le lundi.
4. Ils ______________ (regarder) la télé.
5. Je ______________ (jouer) au tennis avec Denise.
6. Mai ______________ (aimer) la natation.
7. Il ______________ (écouter) la radio.
8. Vous ______________ (aimer) faire des photos.

VOCABULAIRE Seasons and time expressions

16 Sébastien is having trouble in French class. Read his work and decide whether each of his answers is logical (**Y**) or not (**N**). If his answer is not logical, correct it.

_____ 1. Il fait très chaud au Canada en hiver.

____

_____ 2. Il ne pleut pas au printemps.

____

_____ 3. On fait du ski en hiver.

____

_____ 4. On étudie en vacances.

____

_____ 5. Le soir, on ne regarde pas la télé.

____

_____ 6. Les étudiants n'ont pas de vacances en été.

____

TROISIEME ETAPE

To make, accept, and turn down suggestions, you may want to use adverbs of frequency.

Grammaire Adverbs of frequency

- To tell how often you do something, you can use these adverbs:

  souvent *(often)*, **quelquefois** *(sometimes)*, une **fois par semaine** *(. . . time(s) a week)*, **de temps en temps** *(from time to time)*, **d'habitude** *(usually)*, **rarement** *(rarely)*, and **ne (n')... jamais** *(never)*.

- Short adverbs usually come after the verb.

  Nathalie fait **souvent** des photos.

- Longer adverbs (adverbs that are made up of more than one word) can be placed at the beginning or the end of a sentence:

  Deux fois par semaine, je fais de l'aérobic.
  Paul fait des photos **de temps en temps.**
  D'habitude, je fais de la natation en été.

- **Ne... jamais,** like **ne... pas,** surrounds the verb:

  Je **ne** joue **jamais** au foot.

17 As you read Fabienne and Odile's conversation, underline the adverbs of frequency. Then, complete the statements that follow in English, telling how often Odile does each activity.

FABIENNE Dis, Odile, tu fais du ski?

ODILE Oui, de temps en temps, surtout le samedi et le dimanche.

FABIENNE C'est cool, le ski. Et tu fais de l'exercice pendant la semaine?

ODILE Oui, je fais du jogging deux fois par semaine, après l'école.

FABIENNE Moi, après l'école, j'aime bien faire du vélo. Et toi?

ODILE Pas tellement. Je fais rarement du vélo. Mais, j'aime bien faire de la vidéo. C'est chouette! Je fais de la vidéo une fois par semaine. Et quand il fait beau, je fais de la natation deux fois par semaine.

FABIENNE Moi aussi! J'aime bien faire de la natation. Et j'adore faire du ski nautique aussi.

ODILE Oui, c'est pas mal, mais en été seulement. L'hiver, moi, je fais souvent du patin.

How often does Odile . . .

1. ski? ______________________________________.
2. jog? ______________________________________.
3. ride her bike? ______________________________.
4. make videos? _______________________________.
5. go swimming? _______________________________.
6. skate? ____________________________________.

18 Check off how often the people below do the activities, according to their answers.

	souvent	une fois par semaine	quelquefois	jamais
1. Je n'aime pas du tout faire de la natation.				
2. Je fais de l'aérobic le lundi, le jeudi et le samedi.				
3. Je fais du théâtre le dimanche.				
4. Je fais du ski nautique en vacances.				

19 Sabine is telling what she and her friends enjoy doing. Rewrite her statements, adding the adverb in parentheses in the correct position to tell how often they do the activities.

1. Michel fait de la natation. (souvent)

____

2. Moi, je joue aux cartes. (de temps en temps)

____

3. Laurent joue au golf. (une fois par semaine)

____

4. Mon frère fait du roller en ligne. (ne... jamais)

____

20 Now, tell your pen pal about the activities you and your friends enjoy. Name four of these activities and tell how often you do them and under what weather conditions.

jouer faire	natation ski jogging photos jeux vidéo	foot aérobic patin volley base-ball	souvent quelquefois ... fois par semaine ne... jamais	quand il	fait frais fait froid neige fait chaud fait beau

1. ____

____

2. ____

____

3. ____

____

4. ____

____

Nom ______________________ Classe ______________ Date ______________

On va au café?

PREMIERE ETAPE

To make a recommendation in a café, you'll need to use café foods and beverages and the verb **prendre**.

VOCABULAIRE Café foods and beverages

1 Isabelle and her friends are discussing what to order at the café. Underline the drinks and circle the foods they discuss. Then match the people with what they order.

ISABELLE J'ai très soif. Je voudrais une eau minérale.
ARNAUD Moi, j'ai super faim. Je voudrais un steak-frites.
ISABELLE Tu n'as pas soif?
ARNAUD Si, je vais aussi prendre un sirop de fraise à l'eau. Et toi, Sébastien?
SEBASTIEN Je voudrais juste un chocolat. Je n'ai pas très faim.
CATHERINE Moi, si! Je voudrais un sandwich au jambon et un jus d'orange.
FRANÇOIS Bonne idée! Moi, je vais prendre un sandwich au fromage et un coca.

_______ 1. Arnaud
_______ 2. Isabelle
_______ 3. Catherine
_______ 4. Sébastien
_______ 5. François

a. steak and fries and water with strawberry syrup
b. cheese sandwich and soda
c. ham sandwich and apple juice
d. mineral water
e. cheese sandwich and orange juice
f. ham sandwich and orange juice
g. hot chocolate

2 Unscramble the items below. Then tell whether each item is something you **drink** or something you **eat.**

1. ENU HIECUQ ______________________

____

2. NU WSDHNACI UA GEORMFA ______________________

____

3. NU SUJ ED MEPOM ______________________

____

4. NU EQCORU-NSUMEIOR ______________________

____

3 You're working in a French café during the summer. Create your menu by placing each of these foods and beverages in the proper category on the menu.

limonade — quiche — jus de pomme — steak-frites — hot-dog — omelette — eau minérale — café — sandwich au saucisson — sandwich au jambon — jus d'orange

SANDWICHES	BOISSONS FROIDES *(COLD)*
______________	______________
______________	______________
______________	______________
______________	______________
PLATS (MAIN DISHES)	**BOISSONS CHAUDES *(HOT)***
______________	______________
______________	______________
______________	______________
______________	______________

4 The chef has asked you to help out with the menu. Can you think of an additional item to add to each category? (Don't forget the foods you learned in Chapter 1 !)

SANDWICHES ______________

PLATS ______________

BOISSONS FROIDES ______________

BOISSONS CHAUDES ______________

5 You're at a café with some friends who aren't sure what to order. Make suggestions to them, based on what they like.

EXAMPLE Cara and Claudine like cheese. Prenez des sandwiches au fromage.

1. Malika likes fruit juice. ______________
2. Sylvain and Marie like salami. ______________
3. Liliane likes meat and potatoes. ______________
4. Thi and Jules like grilled sandwiches. ______________
5. Benoît likes hot drinks. ______________

Grammaire The verb **prendre**

The irregular verb **prendre** means *to take* or *to have food or drink (while ordering in a restaurant).* Here are its forms:

je	**prends**	nous	**prenons**
tu	**prends**	vous	**prenez**
il/elle/on	**prend**	ils/elles	**prennent**

Notice that in the **ils/elles** form of the verb, you double the **n.**

6 Barka can't decide what to order, so she asks her friends what they're having. Complete their conversation with the correct forms of the verb **prendre**.

— Simone, qu'est-ce que tu **(1)** ______________?

— Un steak-frites. J'ai très faim!

— Et Arnaud, qu'est-ce qu'il **(2)** ______________?

— Un sandwich au fromage.

— Moi, je n'aime pas trop les sandwiches.

— Hugues et Sandrine **(3)** ______________ toujours des hot-dogs. Ils sont très bons ici.

— Oui, tiens, c'est une bonne idée. Alors, c'est décidé, je **(4)** ______________ aussi un hot-dog. Et comme boisson, qu'est-ce que vous **(5)** ______________, vous?

— Nous **(6)** ______________ tous des citrons pressés.

— Bon, moi aussi, je vais **(7)** ______________ un citron pressé.

7 Everybody's trying to be healthy! Tell which food or drink each person chooses from the choices given.

EXAMPLE (un jus de pomme, un café) Micheline prend un jus de pomme.

1. (un sandwich au saucisson, une salade)

   Ali ______________________________

2. (une eau minérale, un coca)

   Patricia ______________________________

3. (des frites, un sandwich au fromage)

   Toi, tu ______________________________

4. (des fruits, des glaces)

   Ton ami et toi, vous ______________________________

5. (des cocas, des jus d'orange)

   Luc et Samira ______________________________

DEUXIEME ETAPE

To get a server's attention in a restaurant and place an order, you may want to use the imperative.

Grammaire The imperative

To make a request, a command, or a suggestion, use either the **tu** or the **vous** form of the verb without the subject:

Prends un hot-dog! **Prenez** un sandwich au fromage!

When you write a command using the **tu** form of an -**er** verb, drop the final -**s**. If the verb is not an -**er** verb, the form doesn't change.

Tu écoutes le professeur. ➔ **Ecoute** le professeur!

Tu fais tes devoirs. ➔ **Fais** tes devoirs!

When you make commands with the **vous** form, the spelling doesn't change.

Vous écoutez la cassette. ➔ **Ecoutez** la cassette!

Vous faites le ménage. ➔ **Faites** le ménage!

8 Are the commands below directed at **a) one of your friends** or **b) more than one of your friends**?

1. ______ Prenez un sandwich au fromage!
2. ______ Ecoute tes parents!
3. ______ Faites de la natation!
4. ______ Prends un coca!
5. ______ Nagez!
6. ______ Parle français!

9 How would M. Lavalier give the following commands if he were talking to only one of his children?

1. Faites du sport! ______________________
2. Ecoutez de la musique! ______________________
3. Prenez des photos! ______________________
4. Regardez la télé! ______________________

10 Imagine you're a French teacher. Use the imperative to tell your students what to do, based on the cues provided in parentheses.

EXAMPLE Robert (faire tes devoirs) Fais tes devoirs!

1. Nadia et Dominique (faire des photos) ______________________
2. Céline (prendre les feuilles de papier) ______________________
3. Arnaud (écouter le professeur) ______________________
4. Koffi et Lucien (prendre un stylo) ______________________
5. Odile et Pascale (parler français) ______________________

Nom ______________________ Classe ______________ Date ______________

TROISIEME ETAPE

To tell how you liked a meal, you'll need to know some adjectives to describe food. To pay the check, you'll need to use numbers.

COMMENT DIT-ON... ? Adjectives to describe a meal

11 You're a restaurant critic writing a review about a new café. You really liked the ham sandwich you ordered, but you disliked the French fries. Would you make the following remarks about **a) the ham sandwich** or **b) the French fries?**

______ 1. C'est délicieux!

______ 2. C'est pas bon!

______ 3. C'est excellent!

______ 4. C'est pas terrible!

12 As you write your restaurant review, list two additional ways to describe the ham sandwich and two additional ways to describe the French fries.

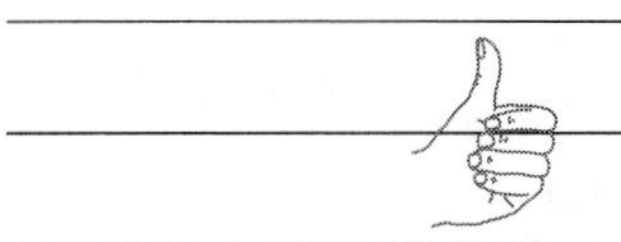

____

____

____

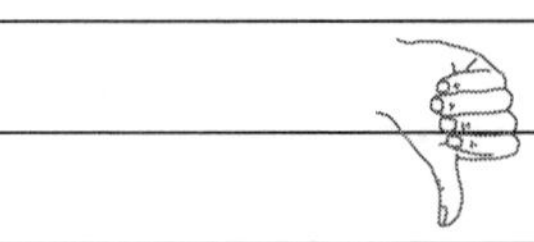

____

____

____

Tu te rappelles? Numbers from 20-100

Here are the numbers from 20–100 in French:

20	vingt	**50**	cinquante	**80**	quatre-vingts
30	trente	**60**	soixante	**90**	quatre-vingt-dix
40	quarante	**70**	soixante-dix	**100**	cent

13 Solve these math problems and write out your answers in French.

1. Soixante-sept moins *(minus)* quarante-deux font *(equals)* ______________________.
2. Cinquante-huit plus vingt et un font ______________________.
3. Quatre-vingt-dix-neuf moins dix-sept font ______________________.
4. Quatre-vingt-sept moins trente-trois font ______________________.
5. Vingt-six plus trente-sept font ______________________.

14 You're a waiter at the Café des Amis. First, add up your customer's checks. Then, write out the totals in French.

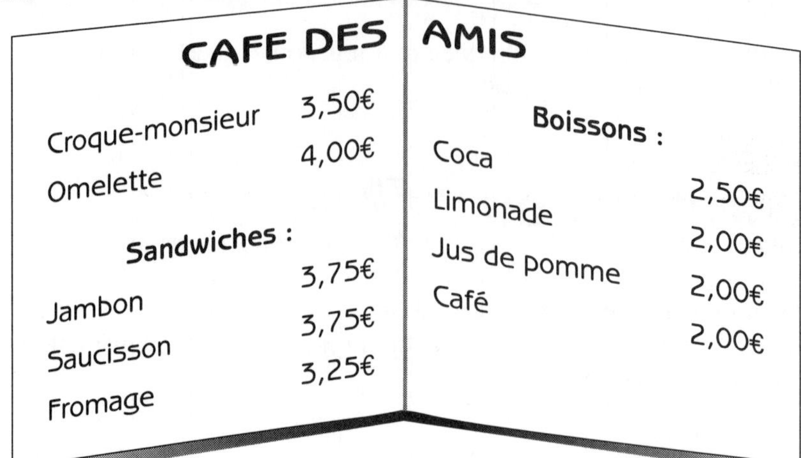

1.
croque-monsieur ________ €
limonade ________ €
________ € ______________________

2.
sandwich au jambon (2) ________ €
café ________ €
coca ________ €
________ € ______________________

3.
sandwich au fromage ________ €
croque-monsieur ________ €
coca ________ €
jus de pomme ________ €
________ € ______________________

4.
omelette ________ €
croque-monsieur ________ €
café (2) ________ €
jus de pomme ________ €
________ € ______________________

Nom ______________________ Classe ______________ Date ______________

Amusons-nous!

PREMIERE ETAPE

To make plans, you'll need to use some activities, the article **le** with days of the week, the verb **aller,** and the names of some places around town.

VOCABULAIRE Activities

1 Marie-Claude and her friends are trying to decide what to do this afternoon. Match each of their remarks on the left with Marie-Claude's suggestion from the column on the right.

_______ **1.** J'adore le sport.

_______ **2.** Je fais du théâtre au lycée.

_______ **3.** J'aime bien faire les magasins.

_______ **4.** J'ai faim.

_______ **5.** J'aime beaucoup le cinéma.

a. On va voir une pièce?

b. On va voir un film?

c. On va faire un pique-nique?

d. On va voir un match de foot?

e. On va à une boum?

f. On va faire les vitrines?

2 Complete this conversation between Olivier and his friends with expressions from the box below.

voir un match	faire les vitrines	voir une pièce	aller à une boum
faire une promenade	manger quelque chose	faire un pique-nique	

OLIVIER Alors, les copains, qu'est-ce que vous faites demain?

HELENE Moi, je vais aller au parc avec mes cousines. On va acheter des sandwiches et des fruits et on va (1) ______________________. Tu veux venir avec nous?

ERIC Bof, ça ne me dit rien. Je préfère aller (2) ______________________ au stade. Montpellier contre Arles. Ça va être super. Et toi, Claudine, qu'est-ce que tu vas faire?

CLAUDINE Je vais aller au jardin du Peyrou. J'ai envie de (3) ______________________ avec mon chien.

MAEVA Moi, je voudrais m'acheter une nouvelle robe pour samedi soir, alors, je crois que je vais (4) ______________________. Et samedi soir, je vais danser. Je vais (5) ______________________ chez des amis.

OLIVIER Dites, vous savez qu'il est déjà midi. On va (6) ______________________ au Café des Trois Grâces?

ERIC D'accord, allons-y.

Note de Grammaire Using **le** with days of the week

Use **le** with a day of the week to say that you do an activity every week on that day.

Le vendredi, je fais du jogging. *On Fridays (every Friday), I go jogging.*

Use the day of the week without **le** to say what you're going to do on a specific day.

Je vais voir une pièce **jeudi.** *I'm going to see a play Thursday (this Thursday, not every Thursday).*

3 Tell whether these teenagers are talking about specific plans for one day or things they do on a regular basis by circling the correct response.

EXAMPLE Prosper «Vendredi, je vais aller à une boum avec Charles.»

(**a.** this Friday) **b.** every week

1. Joëlle «Le lundi, je fais du tennis avec mon ami Gilles.»
   a. this Monday **b.** every week
2. Hamidou «Jeudi, je vais regarder un match de foot à la télé.»
   a. this Thursday **b.** every week
3. Li «Je vais aller à une boum samedi.»
   a. this Saturday **b.** every week
4. Francine «Mardi après-midi, Paul et moi, on va faire les vitrines.»
   a. this Tuesday **b.** every week
5. Xavier «Guillaume et moi, on fait du jogging le dimanche.»
   a. this Sunday **b.** every week

4 Read Karim's letter to Florent. Then underline the activities Karim does on a regular basis and circle the activities he plans to do only once.

Cher Florent,

Je suis désolé mais je ne peux pas faire de vélo avec toi mercredi. Tu sais, je suis très occupé pendant la semaine. Le lundi soir, je joue au foot. Le mardi, je fais de la photo après l'école. Mercredi, je vais à un concert de jazz avec mes parents. Jeudi, je vais au cinéma avec ma cousine. D'habitude, le jeudi, je joue au tennis avec Luc, mais il a un examen de maths vendredi. On peut peut-être faire du vélo ce week-end. Je n'ai rien de prévu pour samedi après-midi. Et toi? Réponds-moi vite!

Karim

Nom ______________________ Classe ______________ Date ______________

Grammaire The verb **aller**

je **vais**	nous **allons**
tu **vas**	vous **allez**
il/elle/on **va**	ils/elles **vont**

- You can use **aller** to tell that you're going to a place.
  Je **vais** au café.
- You can also use **aller** with an infinitive to tell what you're going or not going to do.
  Je **vais étudier** ce soir. Je **ne vais pas étudier** ce soir.

5 Marcelle is writing to her friend Olivia about her plans to visit her friend Yvonne, in Paris. Complete her letter with the correct forms of the verb **aller.**

Chère Olivia,

Ce week-end, je (1) ________ à Paris pour rendre visite à Yvonne. On (2) ________ aller voir une pièce vendredi soir. Les copines d'Yvonne (3) ________ nous retrouver au café après la pièce. Yvonne fait du jogging le samedi. Donc, samedi matin, on (4) ________ aller au parc. Dimanche, nous (5) ________ faire un pique-nique avec Luc, le cousin d'Yvonne. Super, non? Et toi, qu'est-ce que tu (6) ________ faire ce week-end?

Marcelle

6 Tell what four of these people are going to do this weekend.

je Estelle et Monique Mes amis et moi, nous Mon prof de français Fatima	aller	regarder un match à la télé faire les vitrines étudier faire le ménage aller voir un film aller à une boum ???

1. ____
2. ____
3. ____
4. ____

VOCABULAIRE Places around town

7 Lucien won tickets for the football game on Saturday and he's trying to find someone to go with him. Unfortunately, his friends have made other plans. Read their notes and then complete the statements that follow with the correct names.

Désolée, Lucien. Je vais au cinéma samedi soir. —Danielle

Je ne peux pas aller au match samedi soir. Je vais au théâtre avec mes parents. —Bruno

Désolé, Lucien. Je vais au musée avec Stéphanie. —Hugues

Samedi soir, je vais au centre commercial avec des copains. —Alain

1. ______________________ is going shopping.
2. ______________________ is going to the movies.
3. ______________________ is going to see an art exhibit.
4. ______________________ is going to see a play.

8 Answer these questions about Guy's plans for the week in French.

lundi	mardi	mercredi	jeudi	vendredi	samedi	dimanche
aller voir un match	*aller voir un film*	*faire une promenade*	*étudier*	*aller voir une pièce*	*déjeuner avec Mai*	*faire de la natation*

1. Quand (*When*) est-ce que Guy va à la piscine? ______________________
2. Quand est-ce qu'il va au stade? ______________________
3. Quand est-ce qu'il va au théâtre? ______________________
4. Quand est-ce qu'il va au cinéma? ______________________
5. Quand est-ce qu'il va à la bibliothèque? ______________________
6. Quand est-ce qu'il va au café? ______________________

9 Several exchange students will be visiting your area. Tell at least one place they will probably go, in French, based on their interests.

1. Hugues likes to swim. _______________
2. Nathalie likes sports. _______________
3. Marc loves to see plays. _______________
4. Ahmed likes animals. _______________
5. Anne likes shopping. _______________
6. Odile likes movies. _______________

Grammaire Contractions with à

The preposition **à** usually means *to* or *at.* It combines with **le** to form the contraction **au.**

à + le = au Je vais **au** stade.

A combines with **les** to form the contraction **aux.**

à + les = aux Après, je vais **aux** Invalides.

A doesn't contract with **l'** or **la.**

Dimanche, je vais **à la** piscine et **au** stade. Lundi, je vais **à l'**école.

10 Magali and her classmates are telling one another where they plan to go on Saturday. Complete their statements with **à la, à l', au,** or **aux.**

1. Je vais aller _______________ école.
2. Pas moi! Je vais _______________ stade.
3. Moi, je préfère aller _______________ Tuileries.
4. Moi, je vais _______________ Maison des jeunes. C'est plus cool.
5. Et moi, je vais aller chercher des livres _______________ bibliothèque.
6. Je vais voir une pièce _______________ théâtre.

11 Tell three activities you plan to do this weekend and when and where you will do each activity.

EXAMPLE Vendredi soir, je vais voir un match au stade.

____

____

____

____

____

____

DEUXIEME ETAPE

To extend and respond to invitations, you'll need to use the verb **vouloir.**

Grammaire The verb **vouloir**

The irregular verb **vouloir** means *to want.* Here are its forms:

je **veux**	nous **voulons**
tu **veux**	vous **voulez**
il/elle/on **veut**	ils/elles **veulent**

The phrase **je voudrais** *(I would like)*, which you already know, is a more polite form of **je veux.**

12 Complete each statement by selecting the correct subject.

1. ________ voulons regarder un match à la télé.
2. ________ veut voir une pièce.
3. ________ veulent voir un film.
4. ________ veux faire les vitrines.
5. ________ voulez manger quelque chose, non?

a. Moi, je...
b. Didier et Raoul...
c. Nathalie...
d. Et vous, vous...
e. Catherine et moi, nous...

13 Henri is writing a note to his friend to ask for advice about what to do on Saturday night. Complete his note with the correct forms of the verb **vouloir.**

Salut Bruno,

Ça va? Dis, qu'est-ce que tu fais samedi soir? Nathalie (1) ______________ aller à une boum. Georges et Francine (2) ______________ aller au cinéma. Mais Céline, Coralie et moi, nous (3) ______________ faire quelque chose de différent. Tu as une idée? Moi, je (4) ______________ aller au théâtre mais Céline et Coralie n'aiment pas ça. Elles (5) ______________ aller voir un match de football américain. Tu (6) ______________ faire quelque chose avec nous? Téléphone-moi ce soir.

A bientôt,

Henri

Nom ____________________ Classe ____________ Date ____________

TROISIEME ETAPE

To arrange to meet someone, you need to use time expressions and tell time. You'll also need to ask information questions.

COMMENT DIT-ON... ? Days of the week and time expressions

14 Every Monday, Nathalie makes plans for the upcoming week. Complete her planner in English by listing the places she'll go this week, using the information from her journal.

lundi 13 octobre

J'ai beaucoup de choses à faire cette semaine. Aujourd'hui, je vais à la bibliothèque. Demain matin, je vais à la piscine avec des amis. Jeudi matin, je vais au musée avec ma classe. Jeudi soir, je vais au cinéma. Samedi, je vais au centre commercial avec ma mère. On va acheter des baskets et un portefeuille pour l'anniversaire de Papa. Et dimanche, s'il fait beau, je vais faire des photos au parc. Ça va être super!

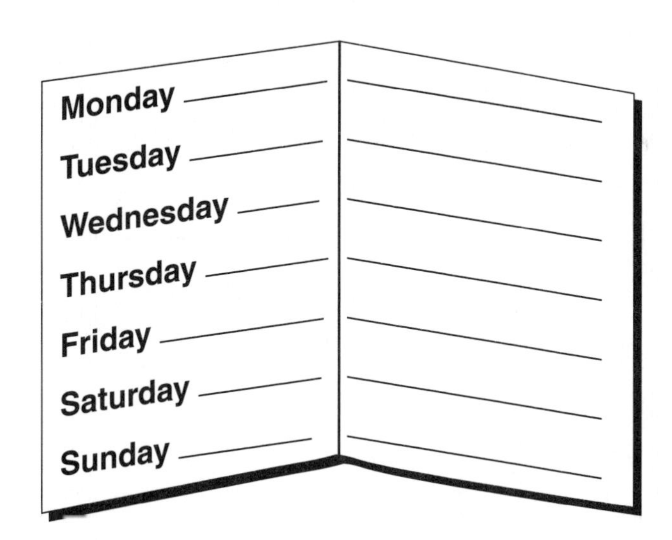

15 Arnaud is making plans to go see a play with Louisa. For each of his questions, circle the response that Louisa wouldn't give.

1. Quand ça?
   a. Demain soir. **b.** Samedi. **c.** Avec Ahmed. **d.** Ce week-end.
2. Où ça?
   a. Tout de suite. **b.** Devant le théâtre. **c.** Chez moi. **d.** Au café.
3. A quelle heure?
   a. A onze heures. **b.** A la boum d'Odile. **c.** A midi. **d.** Vers huit heures.

Nom ______________________ Classe ____________ Date ______________

COMMENT DIT-ON... ? Telling time

16 Serge is supposed to call several French Club members about an upcoming dinner. He wrote down the names and the times, but his notes got mixed up. Number the slips in the order in which he planned to make the calls.

____	*cinq heures et demie – Nathalie*	____	*cinq heures moins le quart – Isabelle*
____	*six heures moins le quart – Jérôme*	____	*six heures et demie – Frédéric*
____	*cinq heures – Rafaël*	____	*six heures et quart – Catherine*

17 Write down the times for each of the clocks you see below.

EXAMPLE  Il est dix heures du soir.

1. ______________________________

2. ______________________________

3. ______________________________

4. ______________________________

5. ______________________________

Grammaire Information questions

- To ask for information, you already know some words to use:

  Où? *(Where?)* **Avec qui?** *(With whom?)*
  Quand? *(When?)* **A quelle heure?** *(At what time?)*

- To ask an information question, you can use just the question word or phrase.

  A quelle heure?

- You can also add **ça** to the end of a question word to make it sound less abrupt.

  Où ça?
  Quand ça?

- Another way to ask an information question is to put the question word or phrase at the end of your statement.

  On va au cinéma **à quelle heure?**

- You can also begin your question with a question word or phrase followed by **est-ce que.**

  A quelle heure est-ce que tu vas au cinéma?
  Où est-ce qu'on se retrouve?

18 You and your friend Sébastien are making arrangements to go to a party. Answer Sébastien's questions based on the invitation.

Vous êtes invité(e)

à une fête

Chez *Charlotte*

Date *samedi 18 octobre*

A *20h00*

— C'est quand, la fête de Charlotte?

— ____

— Où est la fête?

— ____

— A quelle heure commence la fête?

— ____

19 You overhear some people talking on a public phone. Based on what they say, decide what question they were asked.

Quand ça? Où ça? Avec qui? A quelle heure?

1. ______________________ «A huit heures et quart.»
2. ______________________ «Avec Marie-Hélène et Amina.»
3. ______________________ «A minuit.»
4. ______________________ «Devant le stade.»
5. ______________________ «Chez Isabelle.»
6. ______________________ «Demain matin.»
7. ______________________ «A la bibliothèque.»
8. ______________________ «Samedi soir.»

20 Céline and Daniel are deciding where to meet. Complete Céline's part of the conversation with the correct question word or phrase.

— Salut, Céline.

— Salut, Daniel.

— Tu veux aller au centre commercial?

1. — ______________________

— Demain après-midi.

2. — ______________________

— A quatre heures.

3. — ______________________

— Avec Marius, Karine et Nathan. On se retrouve à trois heures.

4. — ______________________

— Au café.

— Oui, je veux bien.

21 You need to call your new French friend to make plans to do something this weekend. Before you call, make a list of three questions you'll need to ask your friend about when and where to meet.

1. ______________________
2. ______________________
3. ______________________

Nom ______________________ Classe ______________ Date ______________

La famille

PREMIERE ETAPE

To identify and introduce people, you might need to know the names of the family members. You'll need to use **de** and possessive adjectives to indicate relationships between people and to show ownership.

VOCABULAIRE Family members

1 Using the information in Alexandre's note, complete the sentences that follow in English about his family.

Salut! Je m'appelle Alexandre Dulac. Ma mère s'appelle Agnès et mon père s'appelle Martin. J'ai un frère, Guy, et une sœur, Patricia. J'ai une tante, Marion, un oncle, Yves, une cousine, Gisèle, et un cousin, Gilbert. Ma grand-mère s'appelle Bernadette et mon grand-père s'appelle Maurice.

1. Martin is Alexandre's ______________________.
2. Marion is Alexandre's ______________________.
3. Maurice is Alexandre's ______________________.
4. Patricia is Alexandre's ______________________.
5. Agnès is Alexandre's ______________________.

2 Fill in the missing letters to complete each of the words below. Then, unscramble the letters that appeared in the bold-faced blanks to reveal another member of Alexandre's family.

1. _ N _ _ **_**
   3 13 1 16 **14**
2. **_** _ _ S **_** _ _
   1 3 10 15 **8** 13 14
3. _ A **_** _ _
   6 5 **13** 6 14
4. _ **_** _ T
   1 **2** 5 6

Il a aussi un ____ ____ ____ ____ ____.

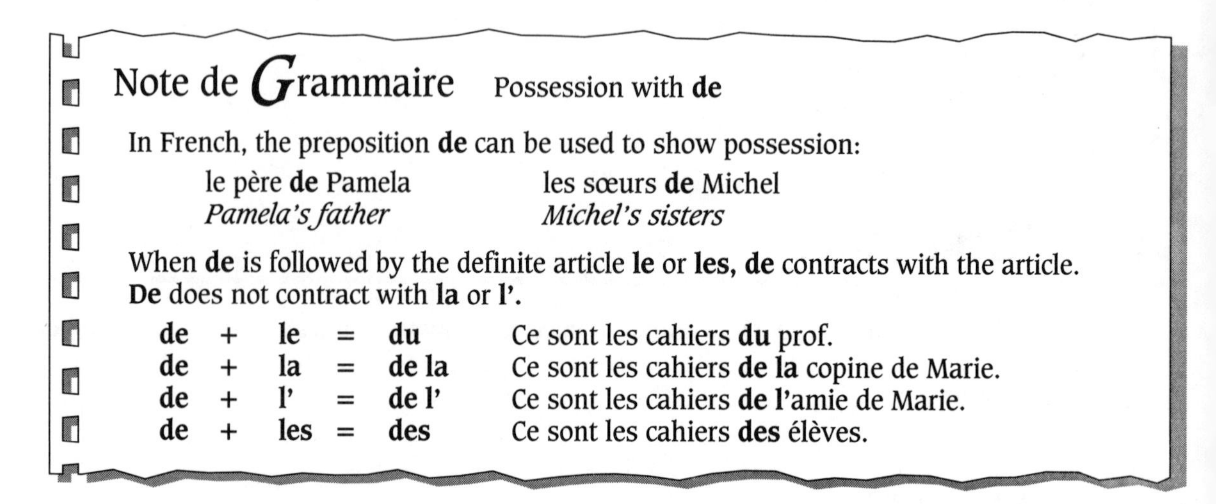

Note de Grammaire Possession with **de**

In French, the preposition **de** can be used to show possession:

le père **de** Pamela	les sœurs **de** Michel
Pamela's father	*Michel's sisters*

When **de** is followed by the definite article **le** or **les, de** contracts with the article. **De** does not contract with **la** or **l'**.

de	+	**le**	=	**du**	Ce sont les cahiers **du** prof.
de	+	**la**	=	**de la**	Ce sont les cahiers **de la** copine de Marie.
de	+	**l'**	=	**de l'**	Ce sont les cahiers **de l'**amie de Marie.
de	+	**les**	=	**des**	Ce sont les cahiers **des** élèves.

3 Tell how these people in Christelle's family are related.

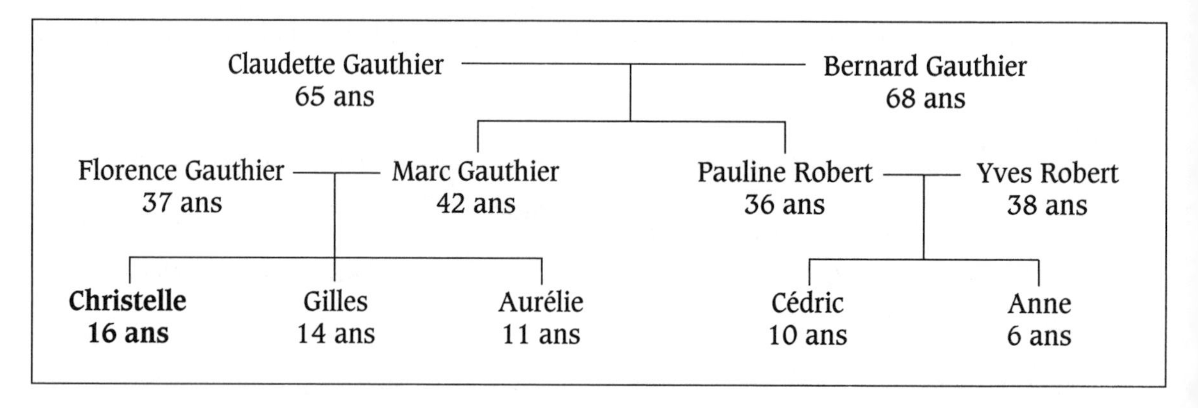

EXAMPLE Marc → Christelle C'est le père de Christelle.

1. Gilles → Marc ______________________________
2. Florence → Christelle ______________________________
3. Claudette → Bernard ______________________________
4. Anne → Pauline ______________________________
5. Yves → Pauline ______________________________

4 Christelle's family reunion is over, and her relatives have all accidentally left things behind. Complete the sentences below with **du, de la, de l'**, or **des.**

1. C'est le tee-shirt ______________ oncle de Christelle.
2. Voilà le vélo ______________ cousine de Christelle.
3. Ce sont les sweat-shirts ______________ cousins de Christelle.
4. C'est la vidéocassette ______________ tante de Christelle.
5. C'est le livre ______________ père de Christelle.
6. C'est le portefeuille ______________ grand-père de Christelle.

Grammaire Possessive adjectives

- Another way to indicate possession is to use possessive adjectives.

my	**mon**	**ma**	**mes**	*our*	**notre**	**nos**
your	**ton**	**ta**	**tes**	*your*	**votre**	**vos**
his/her/its	**son**	**sa**	**ses**	*their*	**leur**	**leurs**

- Like other adjectives, the possessive adjectives must agree in gender and number with what they modify.

  Voilà **mon** sac. *There's my bag.*
  Voilà **ma** trousse. *There's my pencil case.*
  C'est **leur** télévision. *It's their television.*
  Ce sont **leurs** télévisions. *Those are their televisions.*

- Notice that the possessive adjectives **son, sa, ses** mean *his, her,* or *its.*

  C'est **son** ballon. *That's his ball. That's her ball.* or *That's its ball.*

- **Mon, ton,** and **son** are used before any singular noun that starts with a vowel sound.

  Catherine est **son amie.** *Catherine is his/her friend.*

5 Khalid is introducing his family to some of his friends and his teachers. Underline the possessive adjective that correctly completes each of his sentences.

1. Je vous présente (mon, ma, mes) frère, Aziz.
2. Je te présente (mon, ma, mes) mère.
3. Je vous présente (mon, ma, mes) sœurs, Amina et Samira.
4. Je te présente (mon, ma, mes) père et (mon, ma, mes) tante.

6 Priscilla is asking John where his things are. Complete her questions and his answers with the appropriate possessive adjectives.

EXAMPLE

Où est ___ton___ pull-over? ___Mon___ pull est dans l'armoire.

1. Où est _________ auto? _________ auto est dans le garage.
2. Où sont _________ livres? _________ livres sont dans mon sac.
3. Où est _________ vidéocassette? _________ vidéocassette est dans le magnétoscope.
4. Où est _________ dictionnaire? _________ dictionnaire est sur la table.

7 Complete each of the following sentences with the form of the possessive adjective that agrees with the subject.

1. Vous avez _____________ livre aujourd'hui?
2. Nous avons _____________ crayons et _____________ cahiers.
3. Marc cherche _____________ trousse, _____________ classeur et _____________ stylos.
4. Ils aiment _____________ prof de maths.
5. J'aime bien _____________ cours d'histoire et _____________ camarades de classe.

Nom ______________________ Classe ______________ Date ______________

DEUXIEME ETAPE

To describe and characterize people or things, you'll need to use adjectives and the verb **être.** You'll also need to know how to make the adjectives agree with what they describe.

VOCABULAIRE Adjectives to describe people

8 For each of the adjectives listed below, write the word from the box that has the opposite meaning.

âgé	embêtant	brun	intéressant
méchant	grand	blanc	gros

1. blond ______________________
2. gentil ______________________
3. petit ______________________
4. jeune ______________________
5. mince ______________________
6. barbant ______________________
7. amusant ______________________

9 Circle the sentence in the box that does not belong with the other sentences.

1.
Il n'est pas sympa.
Il est embêtant.
Il est difficile.
Il est gentil.

2.
Elle a cinq ans.
Elle n'est pas grande.
Elle est âgée.
Elle est petite.

3.
Je ne suis pas embêtante.
Je suis gentille.
Je suis pénible.
Je suis sympa.

4.
Sa mère est brune.
Son père est blond.
Il est intelligent.
Sa sœur est rousse.

Grammaire Adjective agreement

- In French, an adjective must agree in gender (masculine or feminine) and number (singular or plural) with the noun it modifies. You make the feminine form of most adjectives by adding **-e** to the masculine form. Make the plural form by adding **-s**.

	Masculine	*Feminine*
Singular	Il est grand.	Elle est grand**e**.
Plural	Ils sont grand**s**.	Elles sont grand**es**.

Adjectives like **grand: âgé, amusant, barbant, bleu, blond, brun, embêtant, fort, intelligent, intéressant, méchant, noir, passionnant, petit, vert**

- If an adjective already ends in an **-s,** like **gris,** or an **-x,** like **roux,** you will not add an **-s** in the masculine plural form.

Singular	Il est gris.	Il est roux.
Plural	Ils sont gris.	Ils sont roux.

10 Léa is describing some people. Complete her descriptions, being sure to make any necessary changes to the adjective.

EXAMPLE Mon cousin est amusant. Mes sœurs sont amusantes aussi.

1. Mon père est très intelligent. Ma mère est très ________________ aussi.
2. Ma sœur est blonde. Mon frère est ________________ aussi.
3. Mon amie est très petite. Mes amis sont très ________________ aussi.
4. Mon prof de maths est intéressant. Mes autres profs sont ________________ aussi.

Adjectives ending in -e

If an adjective ends in an unaccented **-e,** the masculine and feminine forms are the same. Make the plural by adding an **-s**.

	Masculine	*Feminine*
Singular	Il est jeune.	Elle est jeune.
Plural	Ils sont jeune**s**.	Elles sont jeune**s**.

Adjectives like **jeune: difficile, facile, jaune, mince, pénible, rose, rouge, timide**

11 Complete each of the sentences below with a logical ending from the list on the right.

_______ 1. Sa fille est...
_______ 2. Mes cousines Lise et Maud sont...
_______ 3. Ton frère est...
_______ 4. Ses frères sont...

a. timide mais amusant.
b. embêtantes et méchantes.
c. jeunes et bruns.
d. blonde et mince.

12 Amina's life is completely opposite from that of her friend Simone. Rewrite Simone's statements so that they are true for Amina.

EXAMPLE Mon chien est blanc. Mon chien est noir.

1. Mon amie est gentille.

____

2. Ma grand-mère est âgée.

____

3. Mes devoirs de français sont difficiles.

____

4. Mon cours d'anglais est barbant.

____

5. Mon petit frère est gros.

____

Adjectives like **mignon**; irregular adjectives

- You double the final consonant of adjectives like **mignon** *(cute)* before you add an **-e** to make the feminine form.

	Masculine	*Feminine*
Singular	Il est mignon.	Elle est mignon**ne.**
Plural	Ils sont mignons.	Elles sont mignon**nes.**

Adjectives like **mignon: bon, gentil, gros, nul, violet**

- Some adjectives have irregular feminine forms that you simply have to memorize, for example, **blanc → blanche** and **roux → rousse.**

	Masculine	*Feminine*
Singular	Il est roux.	Elle est **rousse.**
Plural	Ils sont roux.	Elles sont **rousses.**

13 Write a sentence describing each of these people or cartoon characters. Mention two traits each one has or doesn't have.

EXAMPLE le Président

Il est grand et il est intelligent. OR Il n'est pas âgé et il est intelligent.

1. Garfield® ______________________________
2. ta meilleure amie/ton meilleur ami ______________________________
3. Miss Piggy® ______________________________
4. Wonder Woman® ______________________________
5. Calvin (de *Calvin et Hobbes®*) ______________________________
6. ton professeur de français ______________________________

Invariable adjectives

You don't have to change the form of some adjectives, like **super.**

	Masculine	*Feminine*
Singular	Il est super.	Elle est super.
Plural	Ils sont super.	Elles sont super.

Adjectives like **super: cool, marron, orange**

14 You are writing a letter to a class in France. Describe the following people or animals for them.

EXAMPLE The class clown Il est amusant.

1. The school mascot, an orange and brown dog

____

2. Your two favorite teachers

____

3. Your two best friends

____

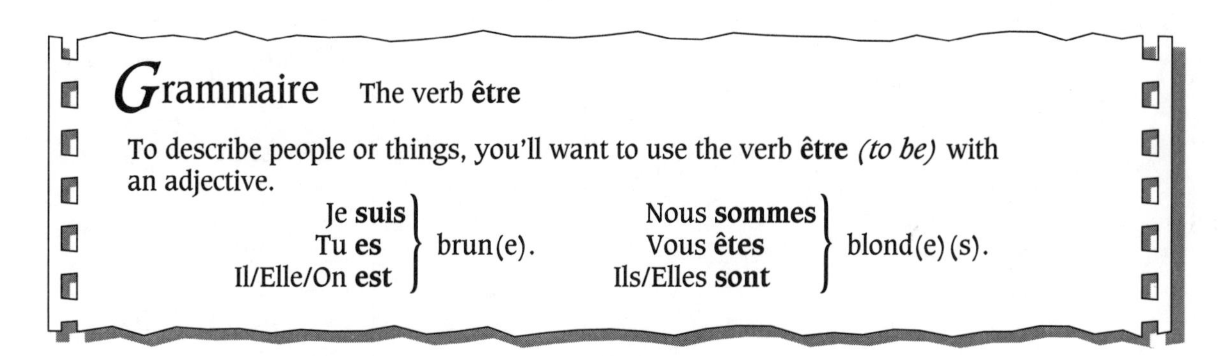

Grammaire The verb **être**

To describe people or things, you'll want to use the verb **être** *(to be)* with an adjective.

Je **suis**	brun(e).	Nous **sommes**	blond(e)(s).
Tu **es**		Vous **êtes**	
Il/Elle/On **est**		Ils/Elles **sont**	

15 Complete the puzzle below with the forms of the verb **être.**

1. je s ___ ___ ___
2. elles s ___ ___ ___
3. nous ___ ___ ___ ___ ___ s
4. tu ___ s
5. vous ___ ___ ___ s
6. il ___ s ___

16 Céline and Ali are talking about their new classmates. Fill in the blanks in their conversation with the appropriate forms of the verb **être.**

CELINE J'aime bien Lien. Elle **(1)** ____________ très gentille.

ALI Oui, et elle **(2)** ____________ mignonne aussi. Paul et Ousmane **(3)** ____________ amusants, mais Paul **(4)** ____________ un peu pénible des fois.

CELINE Oh, tu **(5)** ____________ méchant, Ali!

ALI Je ne **(6)** ____________ pas méchant. **(7)** C'____________ vrai.

CELINE Et qui **(8)** ____________ le garçon roux? Il n'arrête pas de me parler pendant les cours. Il **(9)** ____________ vraiment barbant et ses blagues *(jokes)* **(10)** ____________ nulles.

ALI Et tu dis que je **(11)** ____________ méchant? Tu **(12)** ____________ encore plus méchante que moi.

CELINE Oh là là! Il **(13)** ____________ déjà deux heures. Nous **(14)** ____________ en retard! Allez, viens!

17 Using words from each column, write six sentences describing some of the people in your life and your pets.

Mon Ma Mes	amis chat(te) mère famille sœur(s) père frère(s) copains chien(ne) ??	est sont ne sont pas n'est pas	grand/petit méchant intéressant mince/gros facile/difficile pénible sympathique amusant timide intelligent fort ?? mignon embêtant

1. ____

2. ____

3. ____

4. ____

5. ____

6. ____

TROISIEME ETAPE

To ask for, give, and refuse permission, you may want to know the words for various household chores.

VOCABULAIRE Chores

18 Sylvie asked her classmates what chores they do. Read the results of her survey and answer the questions that follow in English.

	Julien	Fabienne	Olivier	Céline
tondre le gazon		X		X
débarrasser la table	X		X	X
passer l'aspirateur		X		
faire la vaisselle			X	
faire les courses				X
promener le chien	X			
sortir la poubelle			X	
laver la voiture	X			X
ranger ta chambre	X	X	X	X
garder ton/ta petit(e) frère/sœur	X			

1. Which teenagers have to clear the table?

____

2. Which ones have to wash the car?

____

3. Which ones have to vacuum?

____

4. Who has to mow the lawn?

____

5. What chore does everyone have to do?

____

6. What chore(s) does Julien do that no one else does?

____

7. What chore(s) does Olivier do that no one else does?

____

8. What chore(s) does Céline do that no one else does?

____

19 You have a lot of chores to do this weekend! To help you better organize your time, list the chores that you need to do indoors and outside.

sortir la poubelle
passer l'aspirateur
faire la vaisselle
ranger ma chambre
tondre le gazon
promener le chien
débarrasser la table
laver la voiture

INDOORS	OUTSIDE
______________	______________
______________	______________
______________	______________
______________	______________
______________	______________

20 Circle the item in each list that doesn't belong according to its meaning.

1. jouer au foot
   faire du ski
   faire le ménage
   faire une promenade

2. promener le chien
   passer l'aspirateur
   laver la voiture
   tondre le gazon

3. faire les courses
   faire la vaisselle
   passer l'aspirateur
   faire du vélo

4. garder ma sœur
   faire une promenade
   faire les vitrines
   voir une pièce

21 In French, write the chore(s) you associate with each of the objects listed below.

1. a leash ______________________________
2. a vacuum cleaner ______________________________
3. a garbage can ______________________________
4. a sponge ______________________________
5. a lawn mower ______________________________
6. a dust rag ______________________________

Nom______________ Classe__________ Date__________

Au marché

PREMIERE ETAPE

To tell what you need to buy at the market, you'll need to know food items and the partitive articles. You may also need to use the expression **avoir besoin de.**

VOCABULAIRE Food items

1 You're shopping in a market. Place each food item from the box below under the sign where you'd find it.

pommes	poulet	fromage	haricots verts	
fraises	oignons	citrons	goyaves	yaourt
petits pois	ananas	bœuf	beurre	

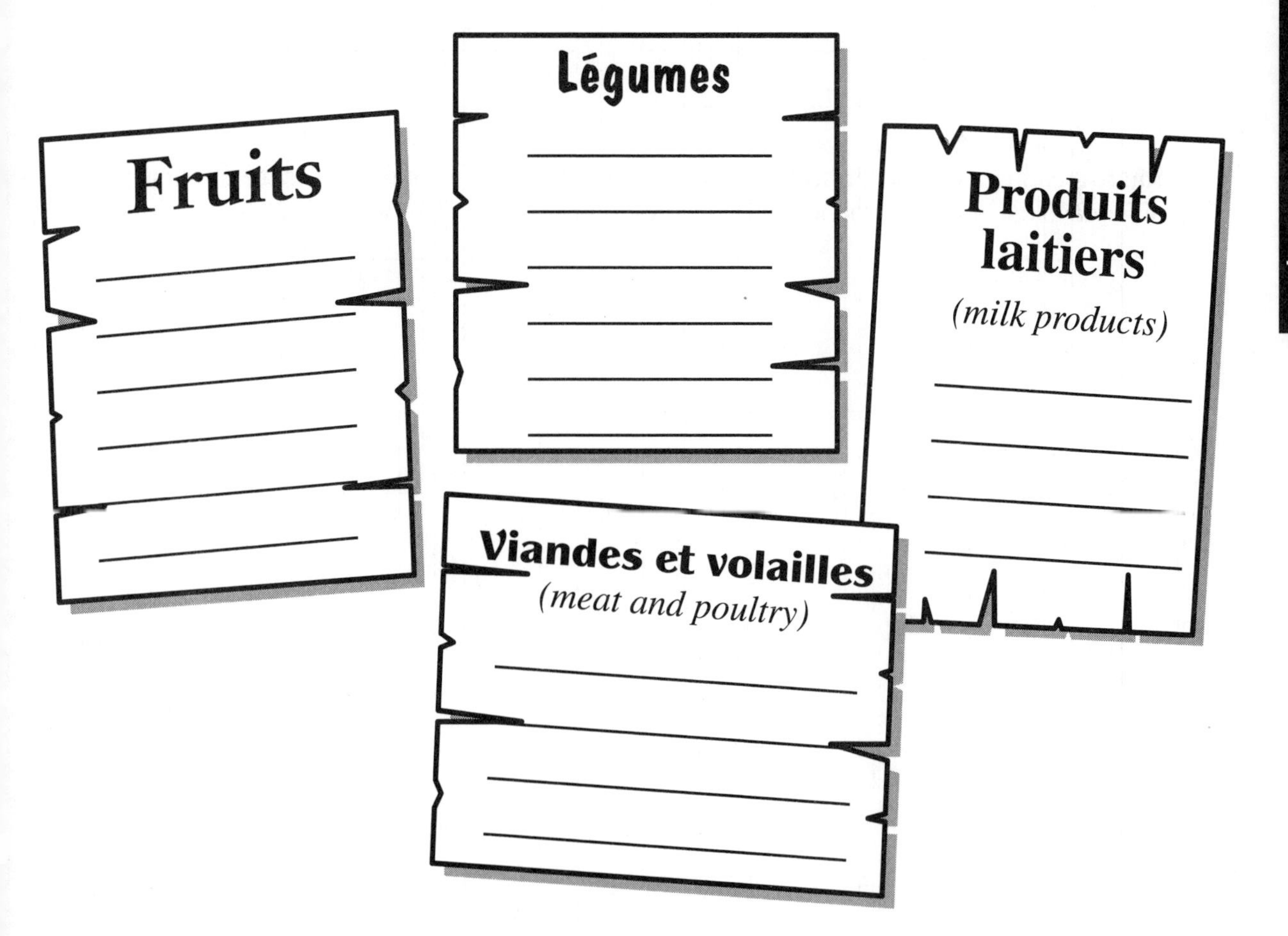

2 Martine is trying out some new recipes. Based on what she would like to make, cross out the item that she will not need.

1. une quiche

   du beurre, des salades, des œufs, du lait

2. un sandwich

   du pain, du fromage, des citrons, des tomates, du jambon

3. une omelette

   des œufs, du fromage, du raisin, des champignons

4. une salade de fruits

   des pommes, des poissons, des mangues, des fraises, des pêches

3 Martine would also like to make a cake. Create a shopping list of the items she'll need to buy in order to make one.

______________________ ______________________

______________________ ______________________

______________________ ______________________

4 You're creating a brochure about fruits and vegetables for health class. Create six illustrations of foods to use for your brochure. Then write the name of each food item in French.

1. ______________________
2. ______________________
3. ______________________
4. ______________________
5. ______________________
6. ______________________

Nom ______________________ Classe ______________ Date ______________

Grammaire The partitive and indefinite articles

- To talk about a whole item or items that are countable, use the indefinite articles **un**, **une**, and **des**.

  Je voudrais **une** tarte aux pommes. *I would like an apple pie.*

  On vend **des** mangues au marché. *They sell mangoes at the market.*

- To talk about *a part of* or *some of* something, use partitive articles. The partitive articles are **du**, **de la**, and **de l'**. In French, you must always include the article, even though you can sometimes leave it out in English.

  Tu veux **de la** tarte aux pommes? *Do you want some apple pie?*

  Mon frère prend toujours **du** gâteau. *My brother always has cake.*

- Both indefinite and partitive articles change to **de** or **d'** in a negative sentence.

  — Tu prends **du** café?
  — Non, je ne prends jamais **de** café.

  — Vous avez **de** l'eau minérale?
  — Non, on n'a pas **d'**eau minérale.

5 Jennifer is having guests at her home for lunch. Decide whether her guests want **a) a whole item** or **b) some of an item.**

1. ______ 2. ______ 3. ______ 4. ______ 5. ______

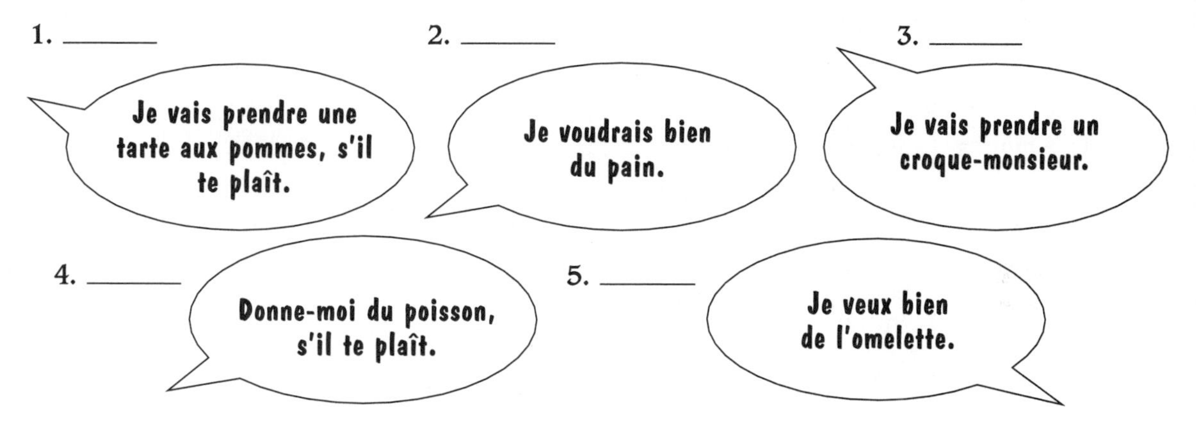

6 Amina's family is telling her what they need at the store. Complete their statements by circling the letter of the correct article.

1. «Amina, tu vas au marché? Il me faut ______ farine pour faire un gâteau.»

   a. du **b.** de la **c.** de l'

2. «N'oublie pas d'acheter ______ fromage! Je vais faire une quiche.»

   a. du **b.** de la **c.** de l'

3. «Achète ______ riz et ______ pain pour le dîner ce soir.»

   a. du, de la **b.** du, du **c.** de l', de la

4. «Amina, il me faut ______ yaourts et ______ confiture.»

   a. de la, de la **b.** de la, du **c.** des, de la

CHAPITRE 8 Première étape

7 Mme Lavalle is leaving her daughter a note to ask her to buy some groceries. Complete her note by filling in each blank with **de, du, de la, de l'**, or **des.**

> *Ma chérie,*
>
> *Tu peux aller au marché après l'école? Il me faut beaucoup de choses. D'abord, il me faut (1) _________ sucre, (2) _________ riz et (3) _________ yaourts. On n'a pas (4) _________ beurre. Tu peux en acheter? Achète aussi (5) _________ maïs, (6) _________ farine et (7) _________ confiture. Ah, j'allais oublier! Achète aussi (8) _________ lait et (9) _________ eau minérale. Merci ma chérie!*

8 Read the shopping lists below and tell what each person is going to buy, using the articles **du, de la, de l'**, and **des.**

EXAMPLE
Louise — bananes, porc, pommes

Louise va acheter des bananes, du porc et des pommes.

1. Aminata — confiture, oignons, haricots verts

____

____

2. Koffi — maïs, citrons, riz, œufs, poulet

____

____

3. Arnaud — beurre, farine, fraises, avocats

____

____

4. Magali — raisin, noix de coco, salades, lait

____

____

5. Martin — bœuf, salades, yaourts

____

____

9 To celebrate your birthday, you're having a dinner party at your house. First, list in French at least five foods you'll serve, including dessert. Then write a note to your parent telling what food items you'll need.

Menu

___

Il me faut ___

Note de Grammaire — Avoir besoin de

To say that you *need* something, you can use **avoir besoin de.** It can be followed by a noun or a verb. The **de** in **avoir besoin de** becomes **d'** when followed by a vowel sound. The partitive article is not used with this expression.

J'ai besoin de lait.

Martine **a besoin d'**ananas.

Vous **avez besoin de** faire des courses.

10 Based on what these people are making for lunch or dessert, tell several items they'll need to buy at the store.

EXAMPLE Charles va faire une quiche. Il a besoin de beurre et d'œufs.

1. Chantal va faire une omelette.
2. Ahmed va faire une salade de fruits.
3. Yamilé va faire un gâteau.
4. Hervé va faire un sandwich.

Nom ________________ Classe ____________ Date ____________

DEUXIEME ETAPE

To make, accept, and decline requests, you'll need to use the verb **pouvoir.** To tell someone what to buy, you'll need to know expressions of quantity and how to use **de** with these expressions.

Grammaire The verb **pouvoir**

The irregular verb **pouvoir** is similar to **vouloir** which you've already learned. It means *to be able to, can,* or *may*. Here are its forms:

je **peux**	nous **pouvons**
tu **peux**	vous **pouvez**
il/elle/on **peut**	ils/elles **peuvent**

11 Find the six forms of **pouvoir** in the puzzle below and write them in the blanks beside the puzzle.

R	P	E	U	M	D	R	T	P	Q
V	P	W	P	G	V	H	Y	A	C
A	S	E	O	Q	V	E	U	X	H
P	I	Q	U	B	D	P	H	G	T
O	P	Z	V	V	P	W	R	N	U
U	L	T	O	H	E	E	R	I	E
V	C	A	N	M	U	N	B	L	P
E	K	L	S	K	X	A	T	L	S
Z	D	X	U	E	P	R	R	D	W
I	N	Z	N	J	V	M	E	B	X

1. ________________
2. ________________
3. ________________
4. ________________
5. ________________
6. ________________

12 Aurélie needs help planning her party. Complete her conversation with Charlotte using the forms of the verb **pouvoir** from Activity 11.

AURELIE Dis, Charlotte, je vais faire une boum chez moi samedi soir. Toi et ton frère, vous **(1)** ________________ m'aider avec la musique?

CHARLOTTE Désolée, je ne **(2)** ________________ pas. J'ai des devoirs à faire. Et mon frère n'est pas là. Tu **(3)** ________________ demander à Patrick.

AURELIE Je lui ai déjà demandé, mais il ne **(4)** ________________ pas m'aider non plus. Il a des trucs à faire.

CHARLOTTE Tu **(5)** ________________ peut-être demander à David et à Suzanne?

AURELIE Oui, bonne idée. Ils ont une chaîne stéréo et plein de CD. Ils **(6)** ________________ sûrement m'aider à choisir la musique.

CHARLOTTE Si tu veux, moi, je **(7)** ________________ t'aider avec les invitations cet aprèm. Nous **(8)** ________________ les faire chez moi.

AURELIE Chouette! Bon, alors, à plus tard.

VOCABULAIRE Expressions of quantity

13 Match each quantity in French with its approximate equivalent in English.

_____ 1. un paquet de sucre
_____ 2. un kilo de pommes de terre
_____ 3. quatre tranches de jambon
_____ 4. un morceau de fromage
_____ 5. deux boîtes de petits pois
_____ 6. une bouteille de coca

a. a slice of . . .
b. a piece of . . .
c. two cans of . . .
d. a bottle of . . .
e. two pounds of . . .
f. a package of . . .
g. four slices of . . .

Note de Grammaire **De** with expressions of quantity

After an expression of quantity, you always use **de** or **d'** before any noun (masculine or feminine, singular or plural).

Il me faut **un kilo de** fraises, s'il vous plaît.
Je voudrais aussi **une bouteille d'**eau minérale.

14 First, unscramble each expression of quantity. Then, find the food item(s) that would most likely be sold in that quantity.

œufs limonade pommes de terre sucre fromage jambon lait petits pois

EXAMPLE NU LKOI ED un kilo de pommes de terre

1. NUE NEADZIUO 'D _______________
2. NU AUMROEC ED _______________
3. NU UTQEAP ED _______________
4. NEU ACEHTRN ED _______________
5. NU ELTRI ED _______________
6. EUN EELLBUTOI ED _______________
7. NEU TOEBÎ ED _______________

15 Some customers are shopping at an **épicerie.** They tell the salesperson what they want, but they don't ask for specific quantities. Rewrite their requests using the quantity given in parentheses.

EXAMPLE «Je vais prendre du jambon.» (une tranche)
Je vais prendre une tranche de jambon.

1. «Je voudrais des pommes.» (un kilo)
____
2. «Des bananes, s'il vous plaît.» (une livre)
____
3. «Il me faut des tomates.» (deux kilos)
____
4. «Je vais prendre des œufs.» (une douzaine)
____
5. «Il me faut du fromage.» (un morceau)
____
6. «De l'eau minérale, s'il vous plaît.» (une bouteille)
____

16 Your parent gave you this shopping list, but forgot to include the quantities! Rewrite the shopping list, including an amount you think you might logically need of each item.

1. des pommes de terre
2. du sucre
3. du jambon
4. du lait
5. des œufs
6. du fromage
7. des haricots verts

1. _______________
2. _______________
3. _______________
4. _______________
5. _______________
6. _______________
7. _______________

TROISIEME ETAPE

If you visit a francophone country, you'll need to know the names of meals. When talking about food, you might also want to know the pronoun **en**.

VOCABULAIRE Meals

17 Some francophone students completed surveys about their eating habits. Based on their responses, decide what questions they were answering on the survey.

a. Qu'est-ce que tu manges au petit déjeuner?

b. Qu'est-ce que tu manges au déjeuner?

c. Qu'est-ce que tu manges au goûter?

d. Qu'est-ce que tu manges au dîner?

______ 1. Après l'école, je mange un fruit.

______ 2. Du pain, du beurre et de la confiture.

______ 3. Je ne mange pas beaucoup le soir. Je mange de la salade ou je me fais une omelette.

______ 4. A midi, je mange des légumes, de la viande et du riz. J'ai toujours très faim!

18 Based on what you've learned about francophone meals, decide whether each of the following meals is **(typique) (T)** or **(pas typique) (PT)**. If the foods listed are not typical for that meal, then rewrite the sentence with the correct meal.

______ 1. Je mange souvent des croissants au petit déjeuner.

____

______ 2. Au dîner, je mange des croissants et du beurre.

____

______ 3. Au déjeuner, je mange du poulet, des pommes de terre et de la salade.

____

______ 4. Au déjeuner, je mange des céréales et du café au lait.

____

______ 5. Au petit déjeuner, je mange du riz et des haricots verts.

____

______ 6. Je mange souvent une omelette et de la soupe au dîner.

____

Grammaire The pronoun **en**

- **En** replaces a phrase beginning with **de, du, de la, de l'**, or **des.** It usually means *some (of it/of them)* or simply *it/them* and is placed before the verb.
  - — Van mange du pain deux fois par jour?
  - — Oui, il **en** mange deux fois par jour.
  - — Vous mangez des fruits?
  - — Oui, j'**en** mange souvent.
- When using **en** in a negative sentence, it means *any* or *none.*
  - — Tu bois du café?
  - — Non, je n'**en** bois pas.

19 Francine loves to eat, but she doesn't like vegetables. Write how she would respond when offered the following foods. Use the pronoun **en** in your answers.

EXAMPLE — Tu veux des petits pois?
— Non merci, je n'en veux pas.

1. — Tu veux des gombos?
   — ______
2. — Tu veux de l'ananas?
   — ______
3. — Tu veux des carottes?
   — ______
4. — Tu veux du gâteau?
   — ______
5. — Tu veux de la viande?
   — ______

20 Benjamin just came back from shopping. His neighbor Jérôme is cooking and needs to borrow a few things. Answer Jérôme's questions based on Benjamin's list. Use the pronoun **en** in your responses.

EXAMPLE Tu as du fromage? Oui, j'en ai.

du lait
du maïs
du sucre
des carottes
du poulet
du fromage
des œufs

1. Tu as du maïs? ______
2. Tu as du pain? ______
3. Tu as des carottes? ______
4. Tu as du sucre? ______
5. Tu as des yaourts? ______
6. Tu as du poisson? ______
7. Tu as des œufs? ______
8. Tu as de l'eau minérale? ______

Nom ______________________ Classe ____________ Date ____________

Au téléphone

PREMIERE ETAPE

To inquire about and relate past events, you'll need to use the **passé composé** with the verb **avoir.** To tell what activities you did and how often you did them, you'll need to know the names of activities as well as where to place adverbs in a sentence in the **passé composé.**

Grammaire The **passé composé** with **avoir**

To talk about what you did in the past, you use a tense called the **passé composé.** It's composed of two parts: a helping verb **(avoir** or **être)** and a past participle.

- The first part, the helping verb, is a present tense form of the verb **avoir** or **être.** Most verbs use **avoir** as the helping verb. Later, you'll learn which verbs use **être.**
- The second part, the past participle, is formed from the infinitive of the verb you want to use. To form the past participle of a verb that ends in **-er,** drop the **-er** from the infinitive and add **-é.**

parler → parlé

J' **ai** / Tu **as** / Il/Elle/On **a** } **parlé** avec Marie.

Nous **avons** / Vous **avez** / Ils/Elles **ont** } **parlé** avec Marie.

To make the negative form of a verb in the **passé composé,** put **ne (n')... pas** around the helping verb.

Sébastien **n'a pas** acheté le CD de Céline Dion.

1 You overhear these remarks in the hallway. Mark **Y** by the statements in which a student is talking about something that happened **yesterday,** and a **T** beside the statements in which a student is discussing plans for **tomorrow.**

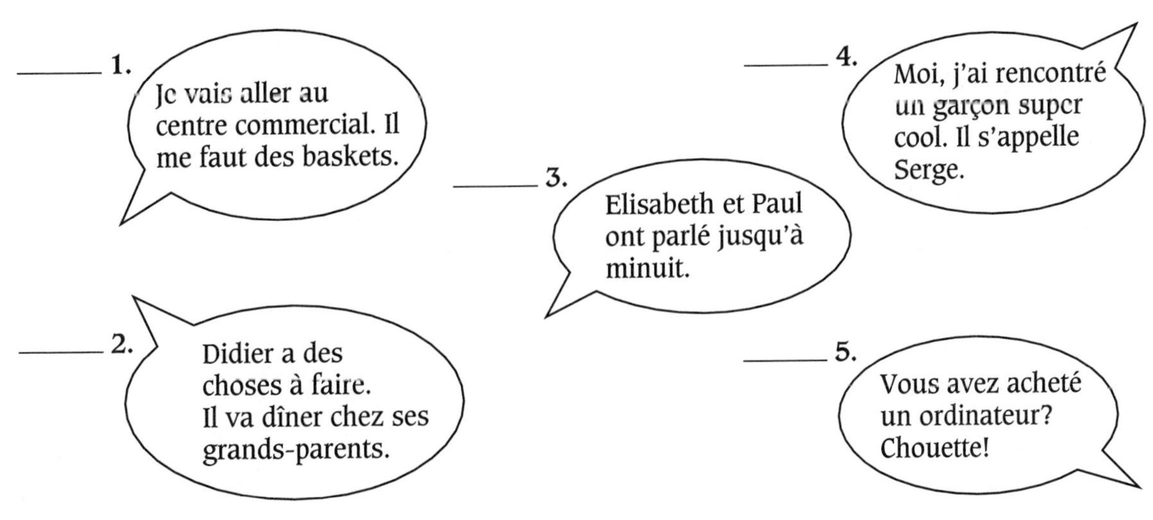

2 Write the correct form of **avoir** in the blank to complete each of the statements below.

________ 1. Martin (ai / a / ont) téléphoné à Suzanne hier soir.

________ 2. Tu (ai / as / avons) parlé à M. Dremière?

________ 3. Caroline! Nous n' (a / avons / ont) pas rangé notre chambre.

________ 4. Marius et ses amis (avons / ont / as) joué au foot cet aprèm.

________ 5. J'ai beaucoup de choses à faire! Je n' (ai / a / avons) pas étudié hier soir.

________ 6. Vous (ai / avons / avez) regardé la télé?

3 Tell what chores David and his family did yesterday afternoon, using the **passé composé.**

ranger passer promener garder
laver débarrasser

1. Moi, je (j') ______________________ ma petite sœur.
2. Ma mère ______________________ l'aspirateur.
3. Mes sœurs ______________________ la voiture.
4. Mon frère et moi, nous ______________________ nos chambres.
5. Mon père, lui, il ______________________ le chien.
6. Ma sœur et mon frère, ils ______________________ la table.

4 Unscramble the fragments to tell what these people did or didn't do last night. Be sure to put the verbs in the **passé composé.**

EXAMPLE écouter / musique / pas / nous / de / ne Nous n'avons pas écouté de musique.

1. voiture / laver / je / la /

____

2. ne / la / Stéphanie / regarder / télé / pas

____

3. leçon d'histoire / étudier / tu / ta

____

4. Philippe / Eva / ne / téléphone / et / au / parler / pas

____

5. pas / promener / chien / vous / le / ne

____

6. vidéo / nous / des / jouer / à / jeux

____

Irregular past participles

Some French verbs have irregular past participles. They don't follow a regular pattern.

Here are some verbs that have irregular past participles:

faire → **fait**		J'ai **fait** mes devoirs.
lire → **lu**		Cédric a **lu** un roman.
prendre → **pris**		Nous avons **pris** un café.
voir → **vu**		Tu as **vu** ce film?

5 Isabelle is writing to tell her pen pal about her weekend. Complete her letter with the correct **passé composé** form of each verb in parentheses.

Chère Djeneba,

Je t'écris pour te raconter mon week-end. Il était vraiment super! D'abord, Didier et moi, on (1) _______________ (prendre) un café. Nous (2) _______________ (parler) jusqu'à deux heures! On (3) _______________ (décider) d'aller au centre commercial ensemble. Nous (4) _______________ (faire) les vitrines tout l'après-midi. Le soir, nous (5) _______________ (voir) un film. C'était super! Et toi, tu (6) _______________ (passer) un bon week-end? Qu'est-ce que tu (7) _______________ (faire)?

Isabelle

6 Julie is finding out what her friends did during their vacations. Complete each statement with **faire, lire, prendre,** or **voir** in the **passé composé.**

— Elodie, tu as passé un bon week-end?

— Non, je (j') **(1)** _______________ mes devoirs.

— Et toi, Raoul, tu as passé un bon week-end?

— Oui, super! Mes parents et moi, nous **(2)** _______________ un bon film.

— Et toi, Nathalie?

— On **(3)** _______________ la voiture de mon cousin pour aller au musée. Et toi, Julie, qu'est-ce que tu **(4)** _______________?

— Je (J') **(5)** _______________ le dernier livre de Stephen King.

7 Gilbert had a fantastic week. Decide whether he did or didn't do the following activities.

EXAMPLE (acheter un CD) Il a acheté un CD.

1. (prendre un café avec des amis) ______
2. (voir un film au cinéma) ______
3. (lire un roman) ______
4. (faire le ménage) ______
5. (jouer au basket-ball avec ses amis) ______
6. (faire la vaisselle) ______
7. (faire du ski nautique) ______
8. (ranger sa chambre) ______

Note de Grammaire

The placement of adverbs in the **passé composé**

When using short adverbs with the **passé composé,** place them before the past participle of the verb. Some of these adverbs are: **souvent, trop, beaucoup, déjà** *(already),* **bien** *(well),* and **mal** *(badly).*

David a **déjà** téléphoné à Catherine. Isabelle a **trop** mangé.

Ne (n')... pas encore *(not yet)* is placed like **ne... pas** and **ne (n')... jamais.** Place the **ne (n')** before the helping verb and **pas encore** before the past participle.

Nous **n'**avons **pas encore** fait nos devoirs.

8 Your great aunt wants to know everything you did this weekend. Answer her questions by placing the adverb in parentheses in the correct position.

EXAMPLE — Tu as mangé au restaurant? (bien) — Oui, j'ai bien mangé.

1. — Tu as téléphoné à ton cousin? (déjà)

   — Oui, ______.
2. — David a mangé hier soir? (trop)

   — Oui, ______.
3. — Vous avez travaillé en classe? (bien)

   — Oui, ______.
4. — Caroline a parlé avec ses amis? (beaucoup)

   — Oui, ______.
5. — Tu as fait tes devoirs? (ne (n')... pas encore)

   — Non, ______.

VOCABULAIRE Daily activities

9 Read about what Bruno did today. Then decide whether the statements that follow are true or false.

> Ma journée a très mal commencé! D'abord, j'ai oublié mes devoirs de sciences nat à la maison. Ensuite, j'ai complètement raté mon interro de français. Mais cet après-midi, tout a changé. J'ai trouvé cinquante euros dans mon sac à dos! Alors, après l'école, j'ai acheté un CD chez le disquaire. Là-bas, j'ai rencontré une fille très sympa. Elle s'appelle Françoise. Le soir, on est allés au café. C'était super!

______________ 1. Bruno had a great morning.

______________ 2. Bruno forgot his homework.

______________ 3. Bruno passed his quiz.

______________ 4. Bruno lost 50 euros.

______________ 5. Bruno met a girl while buying a CD.

______________ 6. Bruno stayed home all evening.

10 Complete these statements with the most logical verb from the box below. Then decide which students had a good day and which had a bad day.

> ai oublié   ai rencontré   ai raté   ai trouvé   ai chanté   ai travaillé

1. Magali : «J' ______________ 20 €! Alors, j'ai acheté un CD.»
2. Mamadou : «J' ______________ mes devoirs de maths.»
3. Karin : «Moi, j' ______________ au fast-food jusqu'à minuit.»
4. André : «J' ______________ une fille super cool.»
5. Margot : «Moi, j' ______________ le bus.»

Good Day	Bad Day
______________	______________
______________	______________
______________	______________
______________	______________

Nom ______________________ Classe ____________ Date ____________

DEUXIEME ETAPE

To make and answer a telephone call, you'll need to know some expressions to use on the telephone. You might also want to know how to form -**re** verbs like **répondre.**

COMMENT DIT-ON... ? Telephone expressions

11 You're creating a guide for tourists to help them use the phone in France. Decide whether each of the expressions below would be useful for someone making a phone call (**M**) or someone answering a phone call (**A**).

_____ 1.
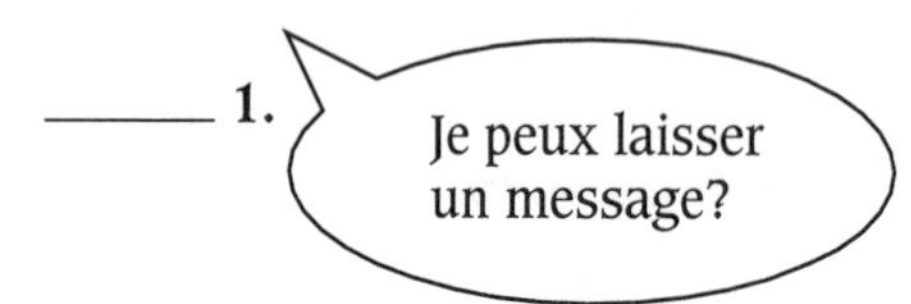

_____ 2.
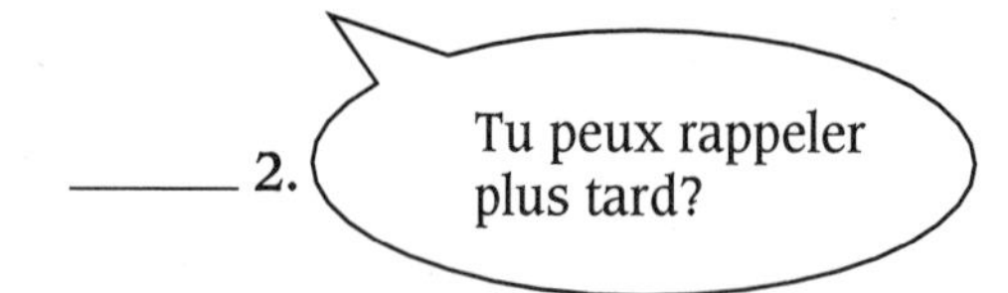

_____ 3.
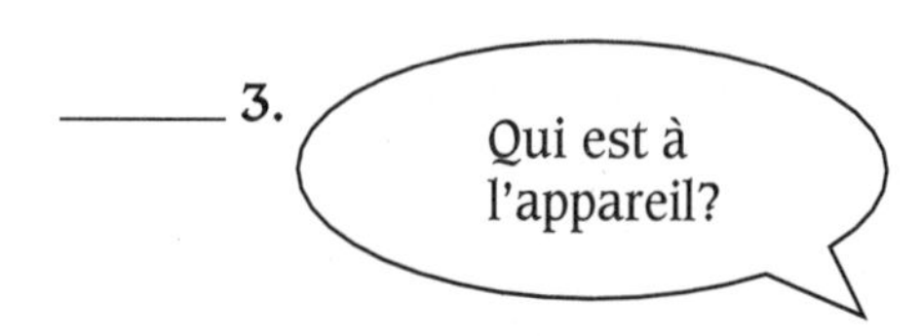

_____ 4. Ne quittez pas.

_____ 5. Ça ne répond pas.

_____ 6. Une seconde, s'il vous plaît.

12 Put the following telephone conversation in order by numbering the lines.

_____ Vous pouvez lui dire que j'ai téléphoné?

_____ Allô.

_____ Une seconde, s'il te plaît... Euh, il est occupé.

_____ Qui est à l'appareil?

_____ Je peux parler à Christian, s'il vous plaît?

_____ Bien sûr.

_____ C'est Nadine.

Nom ______________________ Classe ____________ Date ____________

Grammaire -re verbs

Like -**er** verbs, most verbs that end in -**re**, like **répondre** *(to answer)*, follow a regular pattern. Drop the -**re** from the infinitive and add the appropriate endings:

je répond**s**	nous répond**ons**
tu répond**s**	vous répond**ez**
il/elle/on répond	ils/elles répond**ent**

- Some other -**re** verbs you need to know are **vendre** (to sell), **attendre** (to wait or to wait for), and **perdre** (to lose).
- Use **répondre à** before a noun.
  Je réponds toujours au téléphone.
  Tu dois toujours **répondre** au prof quand il te parle.
- To form the past participle of an -**re** verb, drop the -**re** and add -**u.**
  Nous avons **attendu** deux heures et il a finalement **répondu.**

13 Complete these statements with the correct present tense form of the verb in parentheses.

1. Toi et Frédéric, vous (attendre) ______________ Philippe.
2. Serge (perdre) ______________ le match de tennis.
3. Nous (répondre) ______________ au téléphone quand notre mère n'est pas là.
4. Nathalie (vendre) ______________ son ordinateur.
5. Moi, j' (attendre) ______________ le bus à huit heures le matin.
6. Tu (vendre) ______________ ta radio?
7. Nous (attendre) ______________ Paul devant le lycée.
8. Mai (répondre) ______________ à une carte postale de sa cousine.

14 Create five logical sentences using the past tense and a word from each column. Be sure to make all needed changes.

Toi, tu	répondre	bus.
Michel	attendre	lettre.
Nous	perdre	téléphone.
Elisabeth et Serge	vendre	professeur.
Vous		amis.
Moi, je		livre.
		devant le lycée.
		ordinateur.

1. ______________________________
2. ______________________________
3. ______________________________
4. ______________________________
5. ______________________________

Nom ______________________ Classe ____________ Date ____________

TROISIEME ETAPE

To ask for and give advice, you might need to be familiar with object pronouns.

Note de Grammaire

The pronouns **le, la, les, lui,** and **leur**

- The direct object pronouns **le, la,** and **les** can refer to people or things. You can usually translate them as *him, her, it,* or *them.*

  Il n'a pas téléphoné? Alors, oublie-**le**! *Forget him!*

  Ces baskets sont super. Je **les** prends. *I'll take them.*

- The indirect object pronouns **lui** and **leur** refer only to people and animals. You can usually translate them as *(to) him, (to) her,* or *(to) them.*

  Ecris-**lui** une lettre! *Write him a letter!*

  Pourquoi vous ne **leur** parlez pas? *Why don't you talk to them?*

15 Complete these conversations by circling the correct pronouns.

1. — Je n'aime pas Cédric.

   — Ne (l', les) invite pas à ta boum!

2. — Je n'ai pas vu Charlotte au lycée aujourd'hui.

   — Pourquoi tu ne (lui, leur) téléphones pas?

3. — Je n'ai pas encore fait mes devoirs.

   — Tu devrais (la, les) faire maintenant.

16 Read these statements and circle the person or thing each pronoun is replacing.

1. Tu peux **lui** téléphoner ce soir, non?
   a. Frédéric et Sébastien **b.** Catherine **c.** un téléphone

2. Oublie-**la**!
   a. ton frère **b.** tes copains **c.** ton amie

3. Ecris-**leur** une lettre!
   a. tes parents **b.** tes stylos **c.** ta grand-mère

4. Je ne **les** trouve pas!
   a. tes livres **b.** Simone **c.** ton sac à dos

5. Il est sympa! Invite-**le**!
   a. ta sœur **b.** Jérôme **c.** tes profs

Nom ______________________ Classe ______________ Date ______________

Dans un magasin de vêtements

PREMIERE ETAPE

To ask for and give advice about clothing, you'll need to use clothing items as well as the verbs **porter** and **mettre.**

VOCABULAIRE Clothing

1 Henriette is organizing her closet. Write each item she found in the appropriate category.

une jupe grise — un pantalon noir — une robe bleue — une écharpe rouge
des lunettes de soleil — une casquette verte — une ceinture — des bottes
un maillot de bain — un jean — des chaussures — des boucles d'oreilles

Clothing items	*Accessories and shoes*
______________________	______________________
______________________	______________________
______________________	______________________
______________________	______________________
______________________	______________________
______________________	______________________
______________________	______________________

2 Based on what each person is doing, write the item he or she is not going to wear.

______________ 1. Céline va passer un week-end à la plage.
des sandales — un manteau — un maillot de bain

______________ 2. Arnaud va faire du ski.
une écharpe — une cravate — un blouson

______________ 3. Karine va dîner dans un restaurant élégant avec ses parents.
une robe — des boucles d'oreilles — un short

______________ 4. Koffi va au parc avec ses amis.
une veste — des baskets — un jean

3 What would you wear to the following places? List at least four clothing items or accessories in French for each place.

1. Pour aller à l'école? _______________

2. Pour aller à la piscine? _______________

3. Pour jouer au foot? _______________

4. Pour aller à une boum? _______________

5. Pour aller dans un restaurant élégant? _______________

Grammaire The verbs **mettre** and **porter**

- **Porter** *(to wear)* is a regular **-er** verb.

  Mme Leblanc **porte** une robe bleue. *Mme Leblanc is wearing a blue dress.*

- **Mettre** means *to put, to put on,* or *to wear.* Here are its forms:

je **mets**	nous **mettons**
tu **mets**	vous **mettez**
il/elle/on **met**	ils/elles **mettent**

The past participle of **mettre** is **mis.**

Lucien **a mis** une cravate noire hier soir. *Lucien wore a black tie last night.*

4 Choose the correct subject from the box for each of the statements that follow.

Karim et Joseph	*Jean-Luc*
je (j')	*nous*
vous	*tu*

1. _______________ ai mis une robe grise.
2. _______________ portent tous les deux des shorts et des tee-shirts.
3. Pour aller à une boum, _______________ mettons des jupes et des chemisiers.
4. Et toi? Qu'est-ce que _______________ mets quand il fait frais?
5. _______________ portez toujours des vêtements super cool!
6. _______________ met une cravate noire.

5 Dana and Francine are talking about what to wear to the party this weekend. Complete their conversation with the correct forms of **mettre** or **porter.**

DANA Tu vas à la boum de Cédric samedi soir?

FRANCINE Oui, bien sûr. Et toi?

DANA Oui, moi aussi. Dis, qu'est-ce que tu **(1)** ______________ (mettre)?

FRANCINE Je ne sais pas, mais je voudrais **(2)** ______________ (porter) quelque chose d'original.

DANA Pourquoi tu ne **(3)** ______________ (mettre) pas ton pantalon bleu?

FRANCINE Oh non! Je le **(4)** ______________ (porter) tout le temps, ce pantalon. Je peux peut-être **(5)** ______________ (mettre) ma jupe rouge et mon cardigan noir. Qu'est-ce que tu en penses?

DANA Bof, ta jupe, elle n'est pas très à la mode. Tu devrais demander à Eva de te prêter quelque chose. Elle **(6)** ______________ (porter) toujours des vêtements sensass.

FRANCINE Oui, c'est une bonne idée, ça. Et Florence et Virginie, qu'est-ce qu'elles **(7)** ______________ (mettre)?

FRANCINE Des jeans, sans doute. Tu sais, elles ne **(8)** ______________ (porter) que ça!

DANA Oui, tu as raison. Bon, je dois y aller. A samedi.

FRANCINE Salut.

6 Write complete sentences using the words below. Be sure to use the appropriate form of the verb.

1. mettre / Nathalie / noire / jupe / une

____

2. David / ne / vestes / de / porter / et / pas / Tran

____

3. chemise / je / aujourd'hui / et / porter / une / une / cravate

____

4. maillots / nous / de / mettre / bain / nos

____

5. chaussettes / M. Lagarde / des / porter / bottes / des / et

____

6. tu / mettre / tes / pourquoi / ne / pas / marron / chaussures

____

7. des / pour / mettre / aller / jeans / à / vous / l' / école

____

8. mettre / des / Dianne / Priscilla / robes / et

____

DEUXIEME ETAPE

To choose what you want in a clothing store, you may need to know fabrics, colors, and the verb **choisir.** You'll also need to know how to use adjectives as nouns.

Colors and fabrics

7 Reveal what each customer wants by unscrambling the following colors and fabrics. Then use your results to complete the statements that follow.

David : Est-ce que vous avez des blousons en R I C U ____________?

Martin : Je n'aime pas trop la cravate marron. Vous l'avez en E R G U O ____________?

Sylvie : J'ai acheté un jean et un tee-shirt en N O C T O ____________.

Amina : Je cherche une jupe pour aller à une boum. Vous avez celle-ci en T V R E ____________?

Tran: J'ai trouvé une chemise en N E J A ____________ très cool.

1. ____________ found a denim shirt.
2. ____________ would like a red tie.
3. ____________ bought jeans and a cotton tee-shirt.
4. ____________ would like a leather jacket.
5. ____________ is looking for a green skirt.

Note de Grammaire — Using adjectives as nouns

To use colors or other adjectives as nouns, place **le, la, l',** or **les** in front of the adjective. The article and the spelling of the adjective should agree with the noun you're referring to. Remember, some adjectives never change form.

— Tu aimes les baskets vertes?
— Non, j'aime mieux **les rouges.**

— Tu aimes ce petit bracelet?
— Non, je préfère **le gros,** là.

8 You need some new clothes for school. Write questions in which you ask the salesperson if you can try on the following items.

EXAMPLE une robe verte Je peux essayer la verte?

1. un blouson noir ________________________
2. une jupe rouge ________________________
3. des boucles d'oreilles blanches ________________________
4. une écharpe bleue ________________________
5. des chaussures marron ________________________

Grammaire -ir verbs

- You've already learned how to form **-er** verbs and **-re** verbs. Now, you will learn how to form **-ir** verbs like **choisir** *(to choose)*. To make the stem, drop the **-ir** from the infinitive. Then add these endings:

je chois**is**	nous chois**issons**
tu chois**is**	vous chois**issez**
il/elle/on chois**it**	ils/elles chois**issent**

- The past participle of regular **-ir** verbs ends in **-i**.

  Martin **a choisi** des boucles d'oreilles bleues pour sa mère.

- Here are some additional verbs that are conjugated like **choisir:**

grandir *(to grow)*	Il **grandit** beaucoup en ce moment.
maigrir *(to lose weight)*	Sophie **a** beaucoup **maigri** cette année!
grossir *(to gain weight)*	Si tu manges trop de chocolat, tu vas **grossir.**

9 Choose the correct verb to complete each of the sentences below. Write the letter of your choice in the blank.

1. Vous ____________ le pull orange?
   a. grandissez **b.** maigrissez **c.** choisissez
2. Mon chien ____________ cette année. Il est très grand maintenant!
   a. a maigri **b.** a grandi **c.** a choisi
3. Elles ____________ ces robes-là.
   a. maigrissent **b.** choisissent **c.** grossissent
4. Mon frère et moi, nous ____________ assez facilement, surtout quand nous faisons de l'aérobic.
   a. maigrissons **b.** choisissons **c.** grandissons
5. Est-ce que tu ____________ la robe bleue ou la violette?
   a. grandis **b.** maigris **c.** choisis

10 Complete these conversations with the correct past tense form of the verb in parentheses.

1. — Quelle robe est-ce que tu ____________ (choisir)?
   — J'ai pris la rouge.
2. — Tu vois, mon chat n' ________ pas ________ (grossir). Il est toujours mince.
   — C'est vrai. Mais mon chat, il ________ beaucoup ________ (grossir).
3. — C'est Marc et Li qui ____________ (choisir) la musique pour la fête, non?
   — Oui, ils ____________ (choisir) de la bonne musique.
4. — Oh là là! Tes chats sont si grands!
   — Oui, ils ____________ (grandir) cette année.

11 Complete the puzzle by filling in the blanks below with the correct present tense form of **choisir, maigrir,** or **grossir** as needed.

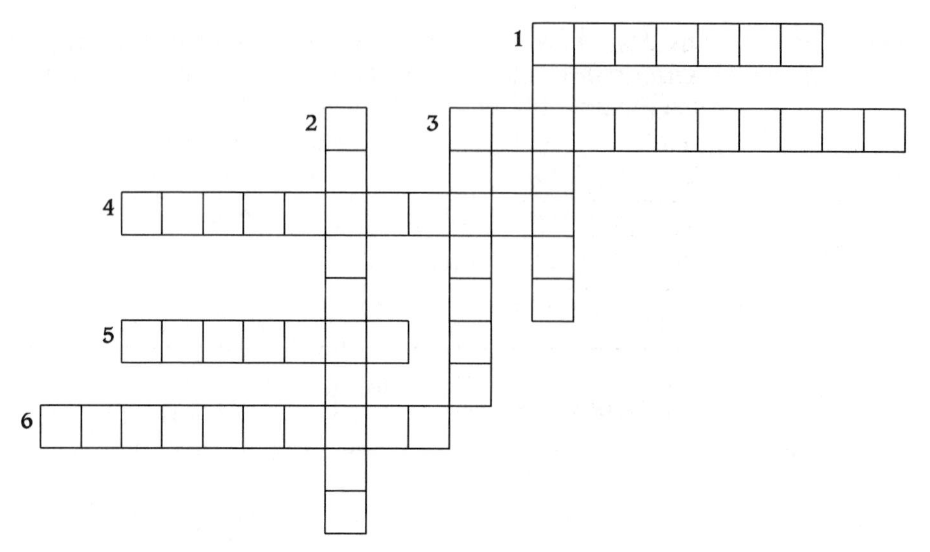

HORIZONTALEMENT

1. Tu manges beaucoup, mais tu ne _______________ jamais! Tu as de la chance!
3. Ils _______________ des manteaux.
4. Céline et moi, nous _______________ ces cahiers bleus.
5. Je _______________ un pantalon à pinces.
6. Vous _______________ la casquette rouge ou la blanche?

VERTICALEMENT

1. On _______________ si on mange trop.
2. Vous _______________ parce que vous ne mangez pas assez.
3. Il _______________ des baskets bleues.

12 Write four complete sentences using elements from each of the boxes below.

Mon chat/Mon chien Ma sœur/Mon frère et moi, nous Moi, je Mes amis Vous Toi, tu	choisir maigrir grossir	ne(n')... jamais. parce que... manger beaucoup. un cardigan jaune. une casquette rouge. les bottes en cuir. un jean marron.

1. _______________
2. _______________
3. _______________
4. _______________

TROISIEME ETAPE

To compliment or criticize clothing, you'll need to know some words to describe how clothes look and fit. You'll also need to know how to use **c'est** and **il est** and the direct object pronouns **le, la,** and **les.**

Complimenting and criticizing clothing

13 You overheard these comments at the mall today. Decide whether each person was **a) complimenting** or **b) criticizing** clothing.

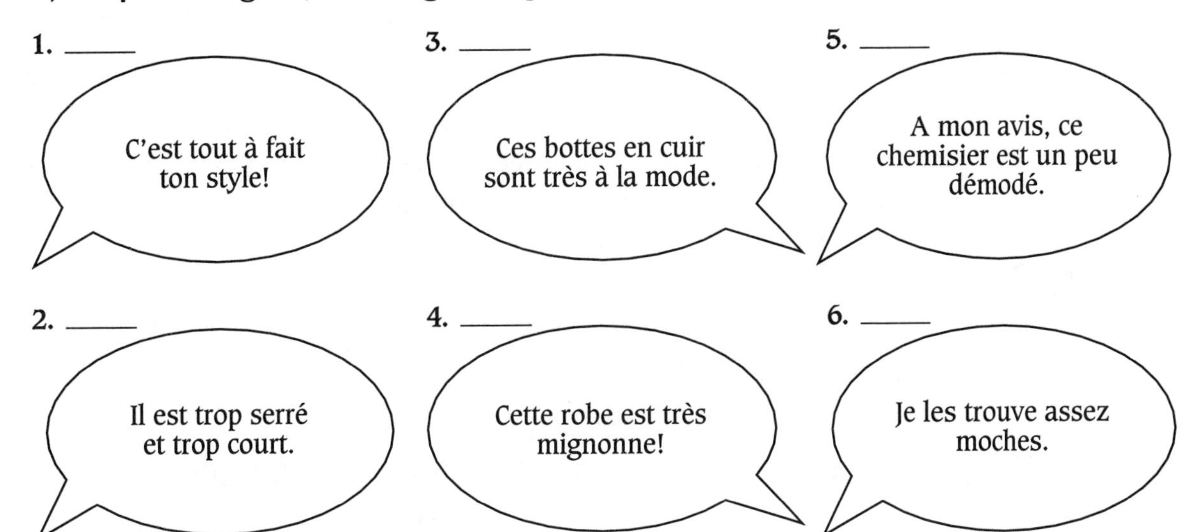

14 Martine and her mother never agree on what to buy. Write what Martine's mother would say about these items, based on what Martine says.

EXAMPLE Cette jupe est trop grande. Mais non, elle est trop petite!

1. Ces bottes en cuir sont très à la mode.

____

2. Cette casquette est sensass!

____

3. Ce pantalon est trop serré.

____

4. Elle me va très bien!

____

5. Ces lunettes de soleil sont horribles!

____

6. Cette robe est très chic, non?

____

15 Your friend Caroline wants to buy a pair of boots you like and a skirt you don't care for. What are two compliments you could give her about the boots? What are two things you would tell her about the skirt?

«Comment tu trouves ces bottes?»

1. ______________________________

2. ______________________________

«Comment tu trouves cette jupe?»

1. ______________________________

2. ______________________________

Grammaire

The direct object pronouns **le, la,** and **les**

- The direct object pronouns **le, la,** and **les** can replace people or things.
  - **Le** means *him* or *it.* — Où est Luc?... Ah, oui, je **le** vois.
  - **La** means *her* or *it.* — Tu veux la cravate? — Oui, je **la** veux.
  - **Les** means *them.* It replaces both masculine and feminine plural nouns.
  - — Nadine aime ces chaussures en cuir? — Non, elle ne **les** aime pas du tout.
- Both **le** and **la** change to **l'** before a vowel sound:
  - — Tu achètes la chemise en jean? — Oui, je **l'**achète.
- **Le, la,** and **les** are usually placed directly before the conjugated verb.
  - Il **la** cherche. Ne **la** prends pas!
  - Je ne **les** invite pas.
- When you have a positive command, place **le, la,** and **les** after the conjugated verb. It is connected to the verb by a hyphen.
  - — Tu aimes cette jupe rose? — Oui, prends-**la**!
- When there's an infinitive in the sentence, place **le, la,** and **les** before the infinitive.
  - — Tu vas acheter ces bracelets? — Oui, je vais **les** prendre.
  - — Clémentine va mettre sa robe bleue? — Non, elle ne va pas **la** mettre.

16 Read the statements below and decide whether the underlined phrase in each one would be replaced with **le, la,** or **les.**

__________ 1. Je vais prendre ce cardigan bleu.

__________ 2. Ah, voilà. Je vois la vendeuse.

__________ 3. Claire choisit ce manteau en cuir.

__________ 4. Si vous allez à la plage, il vous faut ces lunettes de soleil.

__________ 5. Tu cherches Marc et Nathan?

17 You and a friend are shopping for clothes. Respond to your friend's statements, based on the cues. Use the direct object pronouns **le, la, l'**, and **les** in your answers.

EXAMPLE Tu prends ce manteau? Oui, je le prends.

1. Tu achètes cette robe rouge et noire?

   Oui, ____.

2. Tu veux les bottes en cuir?

   Non, ____.

3. Tu vas prendre ces boucles d'oreilles?

   Oui, ____.

4. Tu vas acheter ce maillot de bain?

   Non, ____.

Note de Grammaire **c'est** versus **il/elle est**

- To refer to a specific item, use **il/elle est** or **ils/elles sont.**
  Comment tu trouves ce pantalon noir? **Il est** chic, non?
  J'adore ces bottes noires, mais **elles sont** trop chères.
- To talk about something in general, use **c'est.**
  Je ne mets pas de robe pour aller à l'école. **Ce n'est pas** confortable.

18 Sabine is writing a note to a friend to tell her what she wants to buy at the mall this weekend. Complete her letter by circling the appropriate answers from the choices given.

Danielle,

Je vais au centre commercial samedi. Il me faut beaucoup de choses. Je n'aime plus mon manteau. (1. Il est / C'est) trop démodé. Je vais en acheter un autre. Je vais probablement acheter un manteau en cuir. A mon avis, le cuir, (2. il est / c'est) cool! Je vais aussi acheter une robe verte que j'ai vue la semaine dernière. (3. Elle est / C'est) très chic! Je voudrais aussi acheter un cardigan. (4. Il est / C'est) pratique, un cardigan quand il fait froid. J'ai vu un bracelet très à la mode au magasin Style Chic, mais je pense qu'(que) (5. il est / c'est) trop cher. J'adore le magasin Style Chic. (6. Il est / C'est) vraiment super!

A plus tard!

Sabine

Nom _______________ Classe ___________ Date ___________

Vive les vacances!

PREMIERE ETAPE

To inquire about and share vacation plans, you'll need to know some vacation activities and which preposition to use before cities and countries. To tell what you're going to do this summer, you'll need to use **aller** with an infinitive.

VOCABULAIRE Vacation activities

1 Laurent and his friends are telling each other about their vacation plans. Read their conversation and then complete the sentences that follow.

LAURENT Alors, Dien, tu sais ce que tu vas faire pendant les vacances?

DIEN Oui, en juillet, je vais aller chez mes grands-parents et en août, je pars au bord de la mer, à Biarritz, chez mon oncle et ma tante.

MAGALI Génial! Moi aussi, je vais à Biarritz.

DIEN Tu vas faire du camping là-bas?

MAGALI Non, je vais en colonie de vacances. Ça va être super. On va faire des tas de choses. Et cette année, j'ai décidé d'apprendre à faire de la plongée sous-marine.

DIEN Tu vas voir, c'est génial. Si tu veux, on peut en faire ensemble.

MAGALI D'accord. Et qu'est-ce que tu vas faire d'autre, Dien?

DIEN Je vais faire du bateau et de la planche à voile. J'adore ça! Et toi, Laurent, où tu vas cet été?

LAURENT Moi, je vais aller faire de la randonnée en montagne avec des copains.

SOPHIE C'est super, ça! Vous allez bien vous amuser. Vous allez dormir à l'hôtel?

LAURENT Non, on va faire du camping. Et toi, alors, qu'est-ce que tu vas faire?

SOPHIE Moi, je vais faire un stage de voile, la première semaine de juillet. Et après, je vais aller à la campagne avec mes parents.

LAURENT Bon, alors, bonnes vacances à tous!

1. ______________________ is going to summer camp.
2. ______________________ is going to learn how to scuba dive.
3. ______________________ is going camping.
4. ______________________ is going to visit grandparents.
5. ______________________ is going to the country.
6. ______________________ is going hiking.

2 You're planning your vacation. To decide where you want to go, write the activities you can do at each place, using choices from the box below. Some activities may be used more than once.

faire de la planche à voile | faire de la randonnée | faire de la voile | faire de la plongée | faire du camping | faire du bateau

A la montagne / A la campagne	Au bord de la mer

3 Decide how the first two words in each analogy are related. Then complete the second half of each analogy with one of the choices from the list below.

en colonie de vacances
faire un pique-nique
faire les vitrines
au théâtre
au bord de la mer
faire de la natation
faire de la randonnée

1. au bord de la mer : faire de la plongée :: en forêt : ____________
2. aller chez les grands-parents : à la campagne :: faire du bateau : ____________
3. voir un match : au stade :: ____________ : au parc
4. des baskets : faire de la randonnée :: un maillot de bain : ____________
5. voir un film : au cinéma :: voir une pièce : ____________

4 Your friends are planning their vacations. Based on their interests, tell them where they should go to spend their vacations or suggest some activities they might enjoy.

1. — Cette année, je vais aller au bord de la mer. Qu'est-ce que je peux y faire?

   — Tu pourrais ____________.
2. — Je suis trop stressé! J'ai besoin de calme. Qu'est-ce que tu me conseilles?

   — Pourquoi tu ne vas pas ____________?
3. — J'adore faire du camping. Où est-ce que je peux en faire?

   — Tu pourrais aller ____________.
4. — Nous voulons apprendre beaucoup de choses. Nous adorons les arts plastiques et le sport. Qu'est-ce que tu nous conseilles?

   — Allez ____________.

Nom ______________________ Classe ______________ Date ______________

Tu te rappelles? Aller + infinitive

To tell what *is going to happen*, use a present tense form of **aller (vais, vas, va, allons, allez, vont)** and an infinitive.

Il **va faire** de la randonnée en forêt. *He is going to hike in the woods.*

To tell what *is not going to happen,* place **ne (n')... pas** around the conjugated form of **aller.**

Moi, je **ne** vais **pas** faire de plongée.

5 Vincent and his friends are telling each other about their weekend plans. Unscramble each sentence, using the correct form of **aller.** Then decide whether each person is going to have a good weekend or a bad one.

	Good weekend	Bad weekend
1. jouer / Pascale / tennis / aller / au	________	________
2. examen / Hugues / étudier / pour / et / aller / Robert / un	________	________
3. je / camping / faire / moi / du / aller	________	________
4. randonnée / nous / la / de / aller / faire	________	________
5. tu / le / toi / faire / ménage / aller	________	________

6 Based on their interests, imagine where these people will or will not go to spend their vacation.

EXAMPLE David aime le sport. Il va aller en colonie de vacances.

1. Sabine adore le calme et les animaux.

   Elle ______________________________.
2. Nous aimons faire de la plongée.

   Vous ______________________________.
3. Je veux faire du camping.

   Tu ______________________________.
4. Catherine et Siméon aiment faire du ski.

   Ils ______________________________.
5. Katya veut voir sa famille.

   Elle ______________________________.

CHAPITRE 11 Première étape

Note de Grammaire Prepositions with cities and countries

- Before cities, you usually use the preposition **à:** Ma famille va **à** Paris cet été.
- Before countries, use **en, au,** or **aux** as follows:

Before a feminine country:	Before a masculine country:	Before a country beginning with a vowel sound:	Before a plural country:
en France	**au** Brésil	**en** Israël	**aux** Etats-Unis

- Most countries that end in **-e** are feminine. There are a few exceptions, such as **le Mexique.**

7 Nathalie is writing a letter to her pen pal to tell her about all the places she wants to visit this summer. Complete her letter with the correct prepositions.

Chère Caroline,

Cet été, ma famille et moi, on va faire un super voyage. Je vais aller visiter plein de pays où je ne suis jamais allée. D'abord, en juillet on va prendre l'avion pour aller (1) _______ Angleterre. On va visiter Buckingham Palace (2) _______ Londres. Après, on part (3) _______ Allemagne pour deux semaines. J'adore l'Allemagne! Je veux absolument aller (4) _______ Berlin. Ensuite, en août, on pense partir (5) _______ Italie. J'ai une tante qui habite (6) _______ Rome, alors on va lui rendre visite. Si on a le temps, on va aussi aller (7) _______ Espagne. Il paraît qu'il y a des tas de choses à faire (8) _______ Barcelone. Et pour finir, on va passer une semaine (9) _______ Maroc. Je suis vraiment impatiente de partir. J'aimerais aussi aller (10) _______ Canada, (11) _______ Mexique et (12) _______ Etats-Unis, mais ça ne fait pas partie du voyage. Dommage! Et toi, qu'est-ce que tu veux faire cet été? Tu vas voyager avec ta famille? Ecris-moi vite.

Bisous,

Nathalie

Nom ______________________ Classe ______________ Date ______________

DEUXIEME ETAPE

To remind someone of what they need to bring on vacation, you'll need to know the names of some travel-related items and some weather expressions. You might also want to know the imperative and the verb **partir**.

VOCABULAIRE Items to bring on a trip

8 Find six items in the puzzle below that you would need if you were taking a trip. Then list the six words you found in the blanks beside the puzzle.

K Q W R E W T L V B E L I W N
P Z U O L - N X D F T H U E D
O B I L L E T D E T R A I N M
A S R W M J A T N - O P W B J
R I Q I G R K Z E R P E S H Z
G T D A Z U F - A C E L T Q G
E L - T A Q S N W H S V O F A
N X R E W R I L K J S S T D R
T Z D F O L U D V Q A F S M S
F A P P A R E I L - P H O T O
C O - C F M P G R S M R J X A
R S J N T V A L I S E I O B V
P J W T O I R F X D P L J C W

____
____
____
____
____
____

9 Solve these riddles using the words in the box below.

un billet de train	une valise	un passeport	un cadeau
de l'argent	un parapluie	un appareil-photo	un billet d'avion

1. You need this to fly on an airplane. ______________________
2. Using this will help you remember your trip. ______________________
3. You should bring this back to your family. ______________________
4. You use this to carry your things. ______________________
5. You need this to buy souvenirs. ______________________
6. You would need this to travel outside your country. ______________________
7. You carry this to keep dry in the rain. ______________________

Si tu as oublié... Clothing

10 List at least three clothing items you would pack if you were traveling to these places.

une écharpe | un maillot de bain | un blouson
des sandales | un short | un pull | des lunettes de soleil
des bottes | un jean | un manteau | un cardigan

1. Si tu veux aller en Floride, prends _______________ _______________.
2. Si tu veux aller au Canada en hiver, prends _______________ _______________.
3. Si tu veux aller à Paris en octobre, prends _______________ _______________.

Grammaire The verb **partir**

There are some **-ir** verbs that follow a different pattern from the one you've already learned. **Partir** *(to leave)* is one of these verbs. Here are its forms:

je par**s**	nous part**ons**
tu par**s**	vous part**ez**
il/elle/on par**t**	ils/elles part**ent**

Sortir *(to go out)* and **dormir** *(to sleep)* have the same endings as **partir.**

11 Write the correct form of the verb to complete each sentence.

1. Thi _______________ à huit heures et demie.
   part pars partons
2. A quelle heure est-ce que tu _______________ le matin?
   partent partez pars
3. Michelle et moi, nous _______________ très tard le samedi matin.
   dormons dormez dors
4. Vous _______________ avec vos copains ce soir?
   sortons sors sortez
5. Moi, je ne _______________ pas après onze heures.
   sors sort sortent
6. Omar et sa sœur Larissa _______________ en vacances samedi.
   partent part partons

12 Complete Simon, Charlotte, and Isabelle's conversation with the correct forms of **partir, sortir,** or **dormir.**

CHARLOTTE Tu vas **(1)** _______________ ce soir, Isabelle?

ISABELLE Non, je suis trop fatiguée. Et toi, Simon, tu **(2)** _______________ avec ton frère?

SIMON Non, j'ai trop de choses à faire. Ma famille et moi, nous **(3)** _______________ en vacances demain matin. Nous allons chez mes grands-parents.

CHARLOTTE Chouette! A quelle heure est-ce que vous **(4)** _______________?

SIMON Nous **(5)** _______________ à huit heures du matin.

ISABELLE Qu'est-ce que tu vas faire chez tes grands-parents?

SIMON Mes grands-parents habitent à la campagne; alors, je ne **(6)** _______________ pas beaucoup. Je me couche très tôt et je **(7)** _______________ beaucoup.

Tu te rappelles? The imperative

To make commands, use the **tu** or **vous** form of the verb without the subject.

Prends ta valise! Ne **partez** pas sans votre passeport!

Remember to drop the **-s** from the **tu** form of regular **-er** verbs and **aller:**

N'**oublie** pas ton dictionnaire! **Va** à la gare!

13 Martin and his friends are taking a trip to the Alps to ski with their French teacher, but they aren't ready yet. Tell them what to do to get ready, using the clues given in parentheses.

1. (prendre / un blouson et une écharpe)

   Martin, _______________.

2. (écouter / le professeur)

   David et Christian, _______________.

3. (ne pas oublier / ton argent)

   Patricia, _______________.

4. (acheter / un cadeau pour vos parents)

   Martin et Karim, _______________.

5. (ne pas parler / anglais)

   Patricia et David, _______________.

6. (ne pas oublier / vos valises)

   Sophie et Frédéric, _______________.

7. (aller / à l'aéroport)

   Salimar, _______________.

Si tu as oublié... Weather

14 Choose where each person is going based on the weather reports below.

Alors, aujourd'hui, ceux qui sont en vacances à Nice vont être très contents. Il fait très chaud et tout le monde va pouvoir aller à la plage. Alors, amusez-vous bien et attention aux coups de soleil!

A Paris, toujours du beau temps. Il va faire particulièrement beau aujourd'hui. On prévoit des températures allant jusqu'à 25°C.

Pas de chance pour les vacanciers qui sont en Bretagne en ce moment. Il fait froid depuis le début de la semaine et ça va continuer encore quelques jours. Mais patience, le temps va changer lundi ou mardi.

Pas de soleil pour l'Alsace aujourd'hui. Et oui, malheureusement il pleut à nouveau sur tout l'est de la France. Alors, n'oubliez pas vos parapluies et prudence sur les routes.

_____ 1. Siméon is expecting to get cold weather.
_____ 2. Karima will have hot weather.
_____ 3. It's raining where Philippe is going.
_____ 4. Imelda is expecting nice weather.

a. Alsace
b. Bretagne
c. Nice
d. Paris

15 Based on what these people are wearing or doing, tell what you think the weather is like.

EXAMPLE Ali porte un short et un tee-shirt. Il fait beau.

1. Sabine porte un maillot de bain et des sandales.
____
2. Luc et Jérôme font du ski à la montagne.
____
3. Mes parents font de la plongée.
____
4. Mes sœurs font de la randonnée. Elles portent des sweat-shirts, des jeans et des pulls.
____
5. Nathalie prend son parapluie et elle porte un imperméable *(raincoat)* et des bottes.
____

TROISIEME ETAPE

To ask about someone's vacation or tell about your own, you'll need to use the **passé composé.**

Tu te rappelles? The **passé composé**

- The **passé composé** of most verbs is made of two parts: a present tense form of **avoir** and a past participle.

  The past participles of regular -**er** verbs end in -**é:**
  Il **a parlé** au téléphone.

  The past participles of regular -**re** verbs end in -**u:**
  Martine **a répondu** à la lettre.

  The past participles of regular -**ir** verbs end in -**i:**
  Quel pull **as**-tu **choisi?**

- To make a verb in the **passé composé** negative, place **ne (n')... pas** around the helping verb.

  Je **n'**ai **pas** voyagé cet été.

- Some verbs have irregular past participles:

voir	On **a vu** beaucoup de choses cet été!
faire	Sylvie **a fait** du camping.
prendre	Koffi **a pris** un café.
lire	J'**ai lu** un bon roman pendant les vacances.

- With some verbs, such as **aller** and **sortir, être** is the helping verb instead of **avoir.** When **être** is the helping verb, the past participle agrees with the subject in gender and number.

  Hélène et Patricia **sont allées** en Provence cet été.
  Marie **est sortie** avec ses copains.

You'll learn more about these verbs later.

16 Tell whether these people are talking about what they did last summer **(passé)** or their plans for next summer **(futur)**.

1. Je vais aller à Nice et à Monaco. ______________
2. Tu veux aller à la mer avec nous? ______________
3. Moi, je suis allée à Londres. C'était formidable. ______________
4. Bjan et Laurent sont allés en voyage en Afrique. ______________
5. Ma famille et moi, nous avons fait du camping. ______________
6. Nous allons faire de la plongée à la mer. ______________

17 Sylvie's friends are talking about their vacations. Complete their statements with the **passé composé** forms of the verbs in parentheses.

1. C'était épouvantable! Je (J') ________________ (travailler) tout le temps.

2. Je (J') ________________ (faire) du camping. Et toi? Qu'est-ce que tu ________________ (faire)?

3. Mes frères et moi, nous ________________ (voir) une pièce au théâtre.

4. C'était pas mal. Je (J') ________________ (regarder) la télé et je (j') ________________ (lire) un peu.

5. Alice et ses frères ________________ (voyager) en Europe.

6. Li ________________ (faire) du bateau avec son frère.

18 Using words from each of the columns below, tell what five of these people did last summer.

Moi, je	aller	roman français.
Mes amis et moi, nous	visiter	Floride.
Toi, tu	voyager	grands-parents.
Mon prof	travailler	la tour Eiffel.
Ma sœur/Mon frère	lire	fast-food.
Mes parents	voir	de la randonnée.
	faire	Londres.
		???

1. ____
2. ____
3. ____
4. ____
5. ____

Nom ______________________ Classe ____________ Date ____________

En ville

PREMIERE ETAPE

To point out places and run errands around town, you'll need to use the names of places and tell what you can do at each place. You'll also need to know how to make contractions with **à.**

VOCABULAIRE Running errands in town

1 Lise and her friends are talking about the errands they have to run today. Are they telling **a) where they need to go** or **b) what they need to do?**

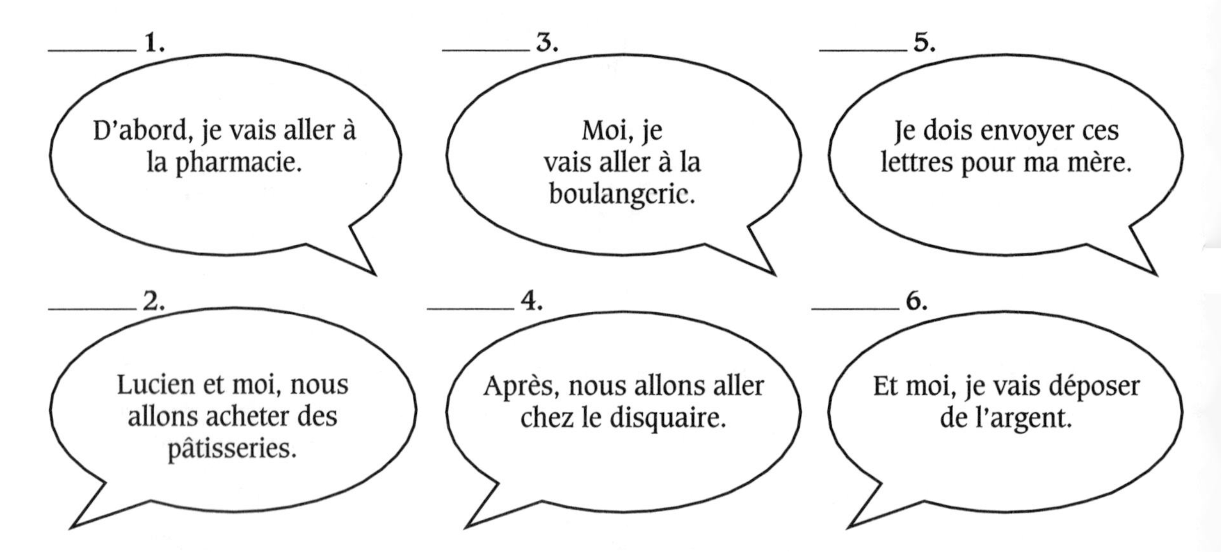

2 Fill in the missing letters to reveal the places Lise needs to go today. Then tell which of the errands from the box below she'll do at each place.

acheter du beurre	acheter des médicaments	déposer de l'argent
rendre des livres	acheter une cassette	acheter des timbres

1. __ O __ T __ ____________________
2. __ P __ __ __ R __ E ____________________
3. __ __ N __ __ __ ____________________
4. __ __ __ __ M __ __ __ E ____________________
5. __ __ __ Q __ __ __ R __ ____________________

3 Dianne can't remember the names of some places in town. Tell her the names of the places in French based on her descriptions.

______________________ 1. C'est l'endroit où on doit aller quand on veut déposer ou retirer de l'argent.

______________________ 2. C'est comme un supermarché, mais c'est plus petit. On peut y acheter toutes sortes de choses, par exemple des fruits, des légumes, de la viande et du fromage.

______________________ 3. Les élèves y vont souvent, surtout à la rentrée des classes. Ils peuvent y trouver toutes leurs fournitures scolaires : des stylos, des cahiers, des classeurs...

______________________ 4. Quand on est malade, on va d'abord chez le docteur. Ensuite, on va dans ce magasin pour acheter les médicaments dont on a besoin.

______________________ 5. On peut y acheter des timbres et des télécartes. On y va aussi quand on veut envoyer un paquet.

4 List all the words you know in French that you associate with each of these places.

LA POSTE

1.

LA BOULANGERIE/PATISSERIE

3.

LA LIBRAIRIE-PAPETERIE

2.

L'EPICERIE

4.

Tu te rappelles? à + the definite article

Au, à la, à l', and **aux** mean *to the* or *at the.* **A** combines with **le** to form **au. A** also combines with **les** to form **aux.**

- Use **au** before a masculine singular noun: → Nathan va **au** centre commercial.
- Use **à la** before a feminine singular noun: → Je vais **à la** poste.
- Use **à l'** before most singular nouns beginning with a vowel sound: → Nous allons **à l'**épicerie.
- Use **aux** before a plural noun: → Tu vas **aux** Etats-Unis? Chouette!

5 Complete Camille and Emmanuel's conversation with **au, à la, à l'**, and **aux.**

CAMILLE Dis, Emmanuel, qu'est-ce que tu vas faire aujourd'hui? Moi, j'ai envie d'aller voir le match de foot (1) __________ stade. Tu veux venir?

EMMANUEL Oui, je veux bien, mais j'ai beaucoup de courses à faire. D'abord, je dois aller (2) __________ épicerie pour acheter de la farine. Ma mère va faire un gâteau.

CAMILLE Pas de problème. On peut faire ça avant d'aller (3) __________ match.

EMMANUEL Attends! Ce n'est pas fini. Je dois aussi aller (4) __________ pharmacie et (5) __________ banque.

CAMILLE Bon, si on allait (6) __________ épicerie tout de suite?

EMMANUEL D'accord. On pourrait aller (7) __________ pâtisserie aussi. J'ai très faim!

CAMILLE Allons-y maintenant! Le match commence à deux heures.

6 Koffi is in town today with his sister Eva. Based on what they're doing, tell where you think they are.

EXAMPLE Ils étudient. Ils sont à la bibliothèque.

1. Koffi et Eva achètent des tartes aux fruits.
____
2. Koffi a besoin de timbres.
____
3. Eva a besoin de champignons pour faire une omelette.
____
4. Koffi n'a pas assez d'argent pour faire ses courses.
____
5. Koffi et Eva veulent acheter trois livres.
____

7 Larissa needs to run errands for her mother. First, make a list in French of the errands she'll need to do, based on her mother's note. Then write where she'll need to go for each errand.

> *Larissa,*
>
> *Je dois travailler toute la journée aujourd'hui et je n'ai pas le temps de faire les courses. Tu peux m'aider? D'abord, il nous faut du pain. Achète deux baguettes. Ton frère voudrait acheter le dernier livre de Stephen King. Tu peux aller le chercher? Si tu as le temps, achète du beurre et du lait aussi. J'ai écrit une lettre à ta grand-mère; il faut l'envoyer. Et comme tu as eu de bonnes notes, tu peux t'acheter un CD. N'oublie pas d'aller retirer de l'argent d'abord. Prends 100 €, ça devrait être assez.*
>
> *Merci!*
>
> *P.S. Ah, j'oubliais! J'ai commandé un gâteau au chocolat pour l'anniversaire de papa ce soir. Passe le chercher!*

acheter deux baguettes	*à la boulangerie*

8 You need to return library books, buy some food at the grocery store, mail letters, and get some cash from the bank. Write a note to your parent, telling what errands you have to run and where you'll have to go to do them. Include two other errands you need to run.

CHAPITRE 12 Première étape

DEUXIEME ETAPE

To make and respond to requests, you may need to use the partitive. You may also need to talk about various means of transportation and use the pronoun **y**.

Tu te rappelles? The partitive

- To say that you want *part* or *some of* an item, use the partitive articles **du, de la,** and **de l'**.
  Je voudrais **de la** tarte aux pommes.
- To say that you want the *whole* item as opposed to *some of* the item, use **un, une,** and **des.**
  Pour le dîner ce soir, il me faut **une** tarte aux pommes et **un** gâteau.
- After a negative, **du, de la, de l', des, un,** and **une** all become **de(d')**.
  Nathalie voudrait acheter **un** disque, mais elle n'a pas **d'**argent.
  Je ne veux pas **de** tarte.

9 You overhear these people telling what they need in the market. Decide whether they want **a) some or part of an item, b) a whole item,** or **c) none of the item.**

_______ 1. «Il me faut du poulet.»

_______ 2. «Oui, je voudrais un gâteau au chocolat et six croissants.»

_______ 3. «Je ne veux pas de fraises aujourd'hui. J'en ai acheté hier.»

_______ 4. «Une baguette, c'est combien?»

_______ 5. «Donnez-moi de la tarte, s'il vous plaît.»

_______ 6. «Il me faut de la confiture.»

_______ 7. «Donnez-moi trois tomates, s'il vous plaît.»

10 Your brother is going into town. Ask him to bring back the following items.

EXAMPLE (some stamps) Tu me rapportes des timbres?

1. (some envelopes) _______________
2. (some medicine) _______________
3. (a cake) _______________
4. (some bread) _______________
5. (an apple pie) _______________
6. (some eggs) _______________
7. (some jam) _______________
8. (a tomato) _______________

Nom ______________________ Classe ______________ Date ______________

VOCABULAIRE Means of transportation

11 You surveyed some teenagers about the means of transportation they like to use. Read the results of your survey and then answer the questions that follow in English.

	à vélo	à pied	en bus	en voiture	en train	en métro	en avion
Amina			X	X	X		X
Elisabeth	X						
Emile	X	X		X	X	X	X
Franck				X			X
Thi	X				X		X
Michèle	X		X		X	X	

1. Who likes to travel by bicycle? ______________________
2. Who likes to walk? ______________________
3. Who doesn't enjoy flying? ______________________
4. Who likes traveling by car? ______________________
5. Who doesn't like traveling by train? ______________________
6. Who likes to use the subway? ______________________
7. Which means of transportation is/are the most popular? ______________________
8. Which means of transportation is/are the least popular? ______________________

12 Find six modes of transportation and write them in the blanks beside the puzzle.

A L K R É T D C D S N I X A T
V O D E H U M V A S O G E D R
I R T A D V B K L O A A M L B
O P L A D V S E M T U B E Y A
N O M H F U A G I N V P M I O
P I L N A B E M C A O G X E V
H T R E M C E R U C E A L N É
H O T E S D G L I T U M Z C L
S A V F R T P I E D M O N O O
B I X M É R V T B U K A E L N
L O I M N V O I T U R E R N P

____
____
____
____
____
____

13 Suggest the best way(s) to travel to each of these destinations.

en métro | à pied | en taxi | en bateau | en bus | en voiture | en avion | à vélo | en train

EXAMPLE de chez toi → à ton école <u>en voiture; en bus</u>

1. de New York → à Paris ______________________
2. de chez toi → au cinéma ______________________
3. de ta ville → à une ville à 200 km de ta ville ______________________
4. de l'aéroport → à l'hôtel ______________________
5. des Etats-Unis → à la Martinique ______________________

14 Unscramble the following means of transportation. Then write a complete sentence telling a place you will go using each type of transportation.

1. NE RITAN ______________________

____

2. EN RVEOTIU ______________________

____

3. NE ONVAI ______________________

____

4. À EDIP ______________________

____

5. NE OMTÉR ______________________

____

6. À OÉLV ______________________

____

15 Complete these statements a travel agent in Paris made yesterday with the appropriate means of transportation.

1. Si vous allez aux Etats-Unis, allez-y ______________.
2. Si vous voulez faire de l'exercice pendant que vous êtes à Paris, visitez la ville

   ______________ ou ______________.
3. Les taxis sont trop chers ici! Allez au Louvre ______________.
4. Versailles? C'est à 26 kilomètres d'ici. On peut y aller ______________.

Grammaire The pronoun y

- To replace a phrase meaning *to, at,* or *in* any place that has already been mentioned, you can use the pronoun **y**. It can replace phrases beginning with prepositions of location like **à, sur, chez, dans,** and **en.**

  Elle va à la pharmacie? Oui, elle y va. / Non, elle n'y va pas.

- **Y** is usually placed before the conjugated verb. If there is an infinitive, place **y** before the infinitive. When using the **passé composé**, **y** is placed before the helping verb.

  — Tu vas à la pharmacie cet après-midi? — Oui, j'y vais.

  — Elle ne va pas à la poste aujourd'hui? — Non, elle va y aller demain.

  — Tu es allée chez le disquaire aussi? — Non, je n'y suis pas allée hier.

16 First, underline the portion of each statement that could be replaced with the pronoun **y.** Then rewrite the statements, replacing the underlined portion with **y.**

EXAMPLE Il me faut de l'aspirine. Je vais à la pharmacie ce matin.
J'y vais ce matin.

1. Je dois envoyer une lettre. Je vais à la poste cet après-midi.

____

2. Non, ne mets pas tes livres sur la table.

____

3. Mohammed et Marie achètent des CD chez le disquaire.

____

4. Cet été, je vais en France.

____

5. Felipe et moi, nous allons à la bibliothèque.

____

17 Hassan's mother is asking him what he did while he was in town today. Write his answers according to his to-do list. Use **y** in your responses.

1. Hassan, tu es allé à l'épicerie?

____

2. Tu es allé à la papeterie?

____

3. Tu es allé à la bibliothèque?

____

4. Tu es allé chez le disquaire?

____

✓ l'épicerie
___ la bibliothèque
✓ la papeterie
✓ la poste
✓ le disquaire
___ le cinéma

Nom ______________________ Classe ______________ Date ______________

TROISIEME ETAPE

To ask for and give directions, you'll need to use location words and contractions with **de.**

Note de Grammaire Contractions with de

- **De** contracts with **le** to become **du** and with **les** to become **des.**
  Before a masculine singular noun, use **du:** La librairie-papeterie est à droite **du** café.
  Before a plural noun, use **des:** C'est près **des** jardins.
- **De** doesn't contract with **la** or **l'**.
  Before a feminine singular noun, use **de la:** La pharmacie est en face **de la** bibliothèque.
  Before most nouns that begin with a vowel sound, use **de l':** C'est en face **de l'**école.

18 A tourist in town is asking M. Lagarde for directions to various places. Complete the conversation with **du, de la, de l'**, or **des.**

LE TOURISTE Excusez-moi, monsieur. Il me faut des timbres et je voudrais aussi envoyer un paquet. Où se trouve la poste, s'il vous plaît?

M. LAGARDE En face **(1)** __________ bibliothèque.

LE TOURISTE Est-ce que la pharmacie est près **(2)** __________ café? Il me faut des médicaments.

M. LAGARDE Non, elle est assez loin **(3)** __________ café, mais elle est près **(4)** __________ banque, au coin **(5)** __________ rue.

LE TOURISTE Au coin de quelle rue?

M. LAGARDE Au coin **(6)** __________ rue Victor Hugo.

LE TOURISTE Bon, d'accord. Et où est le cinéma?

M. LAGARDE En face **(7)** __________ épicerie, à côté **(8)** __________ cafés.

LE TOURISTE Merci beaucoup, monsieur.

VOCABULAIRE Location words

19 Match each location word with its opposite and write your answer in the blank.

__________________ 1. à droite

__________________ 2. loin

__________________ 3. devant

à gauche | en face | près | derrière | au coin

CHAPITRE 12 Troisième étape

20 Aminata isn't familiar with this part of her town, so she asked some people for directions to certain places. Decide whether each set of directions is true **(vrai)** or false **(faux)**, based on the illustration.

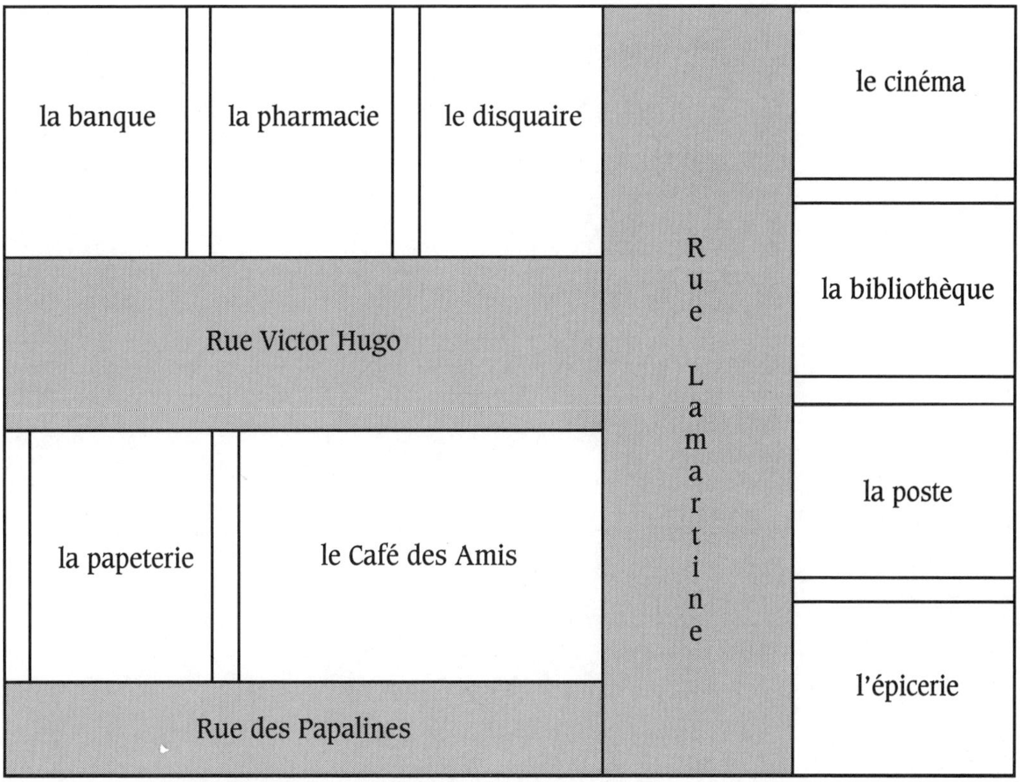

la banque
la pharmacie
le disquaire
Rue Victor Hugo
la papeterie
le Café des Amis
Rue des Papalines
Rue Lamartine
le cinéma
la bibliothèque
la poste
l'épicerie

__________ 1. «Le disquaire est en face de la pharmacie.»

__________ 2. «La bibliothèque se trouve entre le cinéma et la poste.»

__________ 3. «La papeterie est loin du café.»

__________ 4. «La papeterie est à droite de la poste.»

__________ 5. «La poste est à côté de l'épicerie.»

21 Now, it's your turn to help Aminata. Answer her questions about the location of the following places, using the map from Activity 20.

1. — Où se trouve le Café des Amis?

   — ____

2. — Et la banque?

   — ____

3. — Et où se trouve la poste?

   — ____

4. — Je voudrais acheter un CD. Où est le disquaire?

   — ____